Dot.Conned

The Outrageously Funny, 100% True Accounts of Conning Internet Con Men

Diana Grove

Copyright 2009 Diana Grove

ISBN 1448682320
EAN-13 9781448682324
Dot.Conned

All rights reserved. No part of this book may be reproduced, stored in a database retrieval system, or transmitted in any form without written permission by the author except for a reviewer quoting brief passages. This book contains no uranium, polonium, or weaponized beet paste therefore it is safe to ingest, although we discourage it. This book is intended for entertainment purposes only or to stun small rodents. It also makes a great impromptu serving tray for Hubig's pies. May I recommend apple?

Book design and original photography by Diana Grove. Cover design by Mike Gassmann. Photo manipulation by Chrispin Barnes. All other photographs courtesy of Internet con men.

Printed in USA

To buy more copies visit **www.DianaGrove.org**

For Grove,
my partner in crime

Acknowledgments

I'd like to thank the following for their kindness and support:

Susan Schulman and Shelley Schultz for giving me a chance. The Tutton family, Andrei Codrescu, Chris Rose, Don Novello, Mike Gassmann, Tom Purcell, Tom Johnson, Bill Chott, James Finn Garner, The Yes Men, Dan Burt, Octavia Books, Uptown Costume, Langenstein's Supermarket, Rick's Auto Salvage, The McKendrick-Breaux House, Wig World, St. Vincent's Infant Asylum, Majestic Mortuary Service, Chrispin Barnes for his Photoshop work, my friends at Mojo Coffee House, the city of New Orleans - a place I love so much, and all of the con men out there that made this book possible. Keep trying, maybe you'll get me someday.

I'd especially like to thank Todd Grove for his editing, impromptu strategy sessions and unlimited support (and for walking around town in a platinum wig and jump suit).

Contents

Foreword by Andrei Codrescu.....9

Introduction.....11

1. Svetlana Petrokov.....13

2. Fudgey Carmichael.....33

3. Phebus McPhadden.....59

4. Demetrius Chilblain.....79

5. Bradlowe Crumley.....99

6. Dr. Bifida Hendrix M.D.....117

7. Danny Wingnuts.....153

8. Jr. Samples Jr.....171

9. Opus Knight.....179

10. Steve Teufelman.....199

11. Norman Dodd.....217

Notes.....236

Cast and Bios.....242

Foreword

by
Andrei Codrescu

Forget the Da Vinci code. The secret is not in the past, it's in front of you, on the Internet. Diana Grove found it, and she didn't just find it, she actively engaged it, like St. George engaged the dragon. She has proven once again the superiority and virtue of wit, wisdom, and relentlessness over the many-headed evils of scamming the helpless, violating trust, and being cruel to the simple at heart.

I was originally tempted to place Diana Grove's fantastic assumptions of personae within contemporary satirical genres as practiced by Jon Stewart or Steven Colbert. But in reading her flights of fancy, I found them much more powerful. I then thought, reaching into my bag of contemporary action-art, of *The Yes Men*, who assume the personalities of their business targets in order to kung-fu them on their own petards. That would apply in some measure to Grove's characters, who not only accept their apparent roles as victims of Internet scams, but proceed with such enthusiasm that the scammers themselves are in the end overwhelmed. They go places where only surrealist black humor, *pure noir*, ever went before.

The people she invents are brilliant beyond their useful social roles as freakers of scam artists. They are classical literary characters that will last beyond the present incarnation of what we call the Internet. What's great about these action/adventure, real-time stories is that they unfold in an entirely new space continuum, in the virtual world of the global village where no writer has ever been before because the medium is new. The more the predator reacts, the more fantastic the victim becomes - she meets expectations, then surpasses them, then switches roles. The victim becomes the tormentor and the tormentor, who has slowly become addicted to abuse, assumes the victim's role.

So, in addition to being practical, this is also a creative writing and a self-defense manual, a generative text that will make you want to make up your own personae. This is a spiritual collection of stories that demonstrate the potency of good over evil in the most unambiguous spiritual terms.

Oh, and there is sexy, wicked, and perverse writing in here, too, to keep even the most prurient reader on her bright-red toes.

Introduction

There is an old adage - "You can't cheat an honest man." That may be true, but you also can't cheat a girl with a heart full of vengeance and a bag of wigs. And that's what this book is about – vengeance. But it's also about comedy. The following email exchanges detail my 8 month journey beating Internet con men at their own game.

Almost swindled by an online scammer, I decided to give the cops a break and take matters into my own hands. So I answered my spam email – *all of it*. I invented wild fictional characters and went along with their ploys. I had these fraudsters on the hook with the most ridiculous oddballs I could dream up: a six-kidneyed coal miner, a former child star, a quack spine doctor, a murderous taxidermist, and even a schizophrenic ventriloquist. Who needs the Feds when you've got a psychopathic hand puppet on your side?

The result is 246 pages of trickery at its silliest. I hope you enjoy reading this book as much as I had writing it. And remember, it's all 100% true.

Yours in cyberspace,

Diana Grove

Chapter 1.

Svetlana Petrokov

Subject: <u>Svetlana Petrokov</u>
(Former Russian Spy, Job Applicant)
Con Man: <u>Mr. Robert H. Cheng</u>
(Foreign Service Manager for
Jiangsu Tianyin Chemical Company)

Attempted Swindle: <u>$2,000</u>

Subject: IMPORTANT JOB OFFER
From: robcheng_jiangsutianyin@yahoo.com

**Jiangsu Tianyin
Chemical Industry Co., Ltd.**

FROM THE DESK OF JIANGSU TIANYIN CHEMICALS
No.2, Lane 70, Ming Chu Road, Sec.1, Tung Pao, CHINA

This notification is pursuant to request urgent need for a **REPRESENTATIVE IN JIANGSU TIANYIN CHEMICAL COMPANY** based in China.

Over the years we have accumulated invaluable experience in our business and we are proud to claim we are second to none. We aim to be an alert, robust and innovative global company. Suffice to say here, prior to the increase in demand of our products in North and South America and Europe, we have decided to move our products fully into these continents.

We are searching for reliable persons who can act as a **RECEIVING PAYMENTS AGENT** who will act as a medium of reach between our customers and us in their area of locality. Note that if finally approved as our Representative, you are entitled to an annual income of **$24,000 USD** and 10% of whatever amount you receive from customers.

Subject to your satisfaction regarding your interest in being a **"REPRESENTATIVE AGENT"** in the above location and your locality, please send your resume attached via this email: robcheng_jiangsutianyin@yahoo.com

Sincerely,

Mr. Robert Cheng
Foreign Service manager

Tel: +447011133091

**Jiangsu Tianyin Chemical Industry Co. Ltd.
United Kingdom Office
Floor 3 + 4, Newton House
132 New Bond Street
London, W1 S 2nd England**

Subject: Dr. Petrokov Job Resume
From: SvetlanaPetrokov@gmail.com

Dear Mr. Cheng,

I am very interested in your job offer as representative at **JIANGSU TIANYIN CHEMICALS**. I have many years of experience with chemical agents and crowd control substances, particularly dimethyl methylphosphonate, CS gas and weaponized beet paste. Enclosed you will find my photo, resume and job qualifications. I can assure you I would be a loyal servant to your company. Please feel free to contact me day or night, I am at your disposal.

Yours respectfully,

Dr. Svetlana Petrokov

Résumé - Dr. Svetlana Petrokov, Ph.D

Hotel Sovietsky - Rm #331
32 Leningradskii Prospekt Moscow, USSR 125040
7(095)363-2549

Skills: A hard-working chemical specialist with an emphasis in binary munitions and deciduous deforestation. Fields of expertise include mapping wind dispersal, gas dissemination and weaponry in general. A very loyal employee who is trained to work for unlimited hours without food, water, or sunlight and with little or no fresh air. A true-blue worker who will not quit until the job is done then re-done with utmost satisfaction.

Education: Mendeleev University of Chemical Technology (1952-55)
General science degree with an emphasis in Incapacitating Agents and Gastrointestinal Hemorrhaging.

Nikita Krushchev School of Advanced Polytechnics (1955-57)
Advanced degree in Deciduous Deforestation with sub-degrees in Skin Displacement and Acute Bronchospasm.

1996 – 2005: <u>Zardon Chemicals and Bio-Reactionary Institute- Moscow</u>
(Chief Defoliation Expert)

Responsibilities: Researching the expiration of bio-greenery in the Asian Pacific Rim as well as bark dissemination and root liquidation of North America's Great Cedars.

1994-1996: <u>Ministry of Weapons and Foreign Affairs -Spray Tank Division</u>
(Special Agent in Wind Dispersal at Chechen Salt Flats)
Responsibilities: Mapping, tracking and analyzing the dispersal of incapacitating agents with an emphasis in light seizures and loss of consciousness.

1986-1998: <u>Iysocketlosskii Center for Corneal Damage- Chernobyl</u>
(Head of Aberrational Studies)
Responsibilities: Charting detached, reattached and slightly misplaced corneas due to general radiation involvement. Participated in corneal replacement of Minister of Fallout, Victor Noskinski.

1977-1986 <u>Thanatovsky Inc. Vapor Initiative</u>
(Assistant Vapor Advisor and Protective Ointment Specialist)
Responsibilities: Overseeing research and development of Novichok Vapors and CS gas. 1985 - Won medal of honor for inventing gas impermeable body sheath - "The Svetlana Suit 3000" (see photo).

1971-1972: <u>Mortiz and Riggorz Research and Development Project</u>
(Doctor of Engineering and Implementation - Explosives Division)
Responsibilities: Designing and implementing exploding rucksacks for the Lithuanian Student Revolt. Also developed hypergolic pencils with C4 exploding erasers.

1962-1971: <u>Head Nanny for Minister of Energy – Vladimir Popanutz</u>
(Child-Care Specialist/Secretary)
Responsibilities: Maintaining educational control of 3 children aged 1-6 while logging petroleum and natural gas lines of the Greater Siberian Gulch.

1958-1962:   Intensive Study under Grigori Yefimovich Rasputin IV
(Student/Research Assistant)
Responsibilities: Education in the art of mystical transcendence and governmental mind control, plus light housekeeping.

References:
Constantin Churnbludski - Zardon Chemicals 7(495) 233-9680)
Petra Curtainovski - Minister of the Interior – Drapery Division 7(495)254-8597)

The "Svetlana Suit 3000" (patent # 33874)

Subject: GREETINGS MANAGER
From: robcheng_jiangsutianyin@yahoo.com

ATTN: Dr. Svetlana Petrokov,

We at Tianyin Chemical Industry have found you suitable for the job qualification. Concerning your appointment, I am glad to let you know that you are not only going to be our **Representative**, but also our **Foreign Service Manager** at the regional office we intend building in Moscow. This therefore means you are going to be pretty busy. I will send you all you need to do as we proceed. Waiting for your response to this mail.

Sincerely,

Mr. Robert.H. Cheng - Foreign Service Manager

Subject: I Am Very Eager To Begin
From: SvetlanaPetrokov@gmail.com

Mr. Cheng, I am most delighted I have received a promotion even before I have been formally hired by Tianyin Chemical. I can assure you I will work tirelessly to make the regional Moscow office a place of high efficiency. I have already packed up my lab equipment in anticipation of the move.

P.S. I look forward to speaking with you about a top-secret chemical agent I have been working on. Rest assured, if all goes as planned, it will change the world as we know it and nuisances like "revolution" and "freedom of speech" will be a thing of the past.

In eager anticipation

- Dr. Svetlana Petrokov

Subject: Progress Report
From: robcheng_jiangsutianyin@yahoo.com

ATTN: Dr. Svetlana,

Sorry for the delay in attending to your mail, I am always very busy trying to put all regional branches in order.

I want you to know that I am putting up some money to be transfered to you so we can start purchasing the plot along with the materials needed to put a gigantic building in place.

I will get back to you immediately when I am done to tell you how you are going get the funds claimed. Take care my dear partner and friend.

- Mr. Robert H. Cheng

Subject: Special Building Requirements
From: SvetlanaPetrokov@gmail.com

Mr. Cheng, I am glad to hear the building you are planning is going to be "gigantic." As manager of the regional office I must insist we have enough room for a state-of-the art chemical lab and at least 100 research assistants. As I said, I am developing a revolutionary nerve agent that will bring great wealth and recognition to Tianyin Chemical. Allow me to tell you a little about it.

In 1990 I was commissioned by the Russian government to produce a drug called "Apatheron," which was designed to produce a mind-numbing effect useful for crowd control. Unfortunately, it produced an unwelcome side effect of unmitigated weight gain that was found unacceptable by my superiors so I was asked to re-synthesize the compound. As I was busy perfecting the new solution, my husband, Victor Striblitzki, snuck the drug into the hands of top officials in the White House, and with great effect they have been using it on the American public ever since.

Unfortunately, my husband met a tragic end. After beating Henry Kissinger at a game of pinochle he was killed with a radioactive polonium cocktail at the bar of the Hay-Adams. I would say it was a sad day for me but I had my tear ducts removed while working for the Department of Weaponry, so I found it to be mostly an inconvenience.

Mr. Cheng, as long as my new lab is properly equipped, I promise the improved compound, "Apetheron-X," will be far superior to the old version and skyrocket Tianyin Chemical Company to new financial heights. Therefore, I must insist we include in the budget a 50 amp. platinum spectrometer as well as a half a dozen buret clamps and a large supply of human restraint devices.

P.S. This information is top-secret and should not be shared with other parties. Make sure you delete this email immediately and ingest any hardcopies for your own protection. - Dr. Svetlana

Subject: Banking Information
From: robcheng_jiangsutianyin@yahoo.com

ATTN: Dr. Svetlana Petrokov,

Thanks for your urgent reply to my mail. It definitely shows loyalty and seriousness on your part.

Meanwhile, all the sugestions you made regarding the compound "Apetheron-X" will be looked into. I promise you that with the amount of money I am sending, it will cover all the expenses to be made.

At this juncture, I have made available the sum of **$400,000.00 USD** (FOUR HUNDRED THOUSAND UNITED STATES AMERICAN DOLLARS) for transfer via Postbank online in the UK to your desiganted bank account. I therefore implore you to send me your banking details for onward transfer of the said funds.

Please get back to me as soon as possible as I have been trying to get you on the phone to no avail.

I await your urgent reply to this regard.

- Mr. Robert H. Cheng

Subject: Account Information
From: SvetlanaPetrokov@gmail.com

Dear Mr. Cheng,

Regarding a bank account number, I still fear the U.S. government is attempting to hunt me down after the death of my husband, therefore I have been fearful of keeping traceable bank records and have been dealing only in cash. I hope you understand this will in no way affect my working relationship with Tianyin Chemical. I plan to work tirelessly for the company, and considering I had my frontal lobe altered so I require no sleep, this should not be difficult.

In fact, it is because of this delicate situation I am staying at the Hotel Sovietski under various assumed names (i.e.: "Ivinska Tumultikov," "Katrina Abhorikov," and occasionally "Judge Roy Bean"). Ivan, the desk attendant, often does not know which room I am staying in as I change locations every other day to avoid detection.

As you ordered, I opened an account (#009547654-3497721007) at the Bank of Moscow on Rozhdiestvenka Street under the name "Igor Vilanovski." To avoid detection by Agent Y, who I'm afraid is in hot pursuit, I took a circuitous route and disguised myself as a common coal worker. At first I was afraid the prosthetic eyebrows and nose putty would give me away, but apparently bank directors will do anything for 2,600, 000 rubles. (I've included the ID for files.)

P.S. In regards to the new lab, I find it imperative we add on an additional 100,000 to the laboratory budget. I will need that for my primate wing. I currently have 6 retired chimpanzees from the Soviet space program in my hotel room. So far Yuri and Boris are responding well to my behavioral modification program, although last night Boris had an incident with one of the complimentary corkscrews from the mini bar and there was quite a mess. This confirms my previous suspicion - that chimpanzees and potato vodka do not mix. I await further orders.

- Dr. Svetlana (a.k.a. "Agent S")

Subject: Transfer Authorized
From: robcheng_jiangsutianyin@yahoo.com

ATTN: Dr. Svetlana Petrokov,

We are indeed very grateful for your bold step towards the achievements of JIANGSU TIANYIN CHEMICAL INDUSTRY CO. LTD in your country. We are pleased to say that this is a rare achievement and we say thank you in advance. We believe the company's funds are in capable hands, not minding your predicament.

I, as the Foreign Service Manager to this great company hereby authorize the transfer of **$400,000.00** (FOUR HUNDRED THOUSAND UNITED STATES DOLLARS) to the account informations you have provided.

You will recieve a mail from the Account Department of Post Bank UK to this effect. There address is **activation_code@accountant.com.**

I will avail myself in Russia immediately when you get the funds transfered. Reply immediately when you get a mail from the bank.

- Mr. Robert H. Cheng

Subject: I Contacted The Bank
From: SvetlanaPetrokov@gmail.com

Mr. Cheng, as you ordered, I contacted Postbank and gave them my account information. But I apparently owe a $2,000 "cost of transfer" fee to obtain the funds. I do hope they keep my assumed name in the strictest confidence. I wouldn't want to have to use the cyanide lozenge I keep in the heel of my shoe.

That being said, I'm afraid I've had a slight problem with Boris. It seems he's had a bad reaction to Apetheron-X. The new formula is supposed to calm him and make him despondent, but instead he's filled with violent rage and it's taken me three hours just to coax him off the curtain rod. Then he got into my military bag and, as you can see, that's when the trouble really began.

Mr. Cheng, if I don't get his nerves to an appropriate level I'm afraid I'll have to start all over again with my research which could take months with a tremendous increase in budgetary funds.

I can assure you, the Hotel Sovietski is none too pleased with all of the gun fire and clawing at the walls. Is there any way you could call the front desk (7(095)363-2549) and tell Ivan there is nothing to worry about in room 336. There's no way they'll believe I'm a world-famous scientist after I've told them repeatedly I'm a miner for Siberian Coal.

Yours most urgently,

- Dr. S.

Subject: Please Get On Payment...
From: robcheng_jiangsutianyin@yahoo.com

ATTN: Dr. Svetlana Petrokov,

We are sincerely sorry for the problem you are having with your research and we do hope you get it over with very soon. I did call the front desk at the hotel but to no avail as it keeps saying the number is busy.

We ask that you transfer these funds to your bank account right away so that we can start up the company and you could have more money to offset all your bills at the hotel and relocate.

Reply as soon as possible.

Mr. Robert H. Cheng

Subject: Agent Y
From: SvetlanaPetrokov@gmail.com

Mr. Cheng, I must keep this brief as I fear I am in great danger. I spotted Agent Y outside the hotel on Leningradskii Prospect hiding behind a statue of Checkhov. I'm sure it was him because he was looking shifty and talking into his hat. I know this comes at a very bad time as my research is at its apex, but I feel I must leave town for a few days to elude this deadly foe. Believe me Mr. Cheng, the U.S agents will stop at nothing. Agent Y would not think twice about killing me with radiation, anthrax, or even a tainted bowl of borscht. To save myself, I will be disguised as a Polish cobbler and retreat to Minsk. When I feel it is safe, I will return and we can conclude our business.

Because of his recent behavior, I've decided to bring Boris with me. I can now see why he was available at the Space Agency at such a discount. Fortunately, with a little maneuvering, I believe he'll fit quite nicely in my overnight bag.

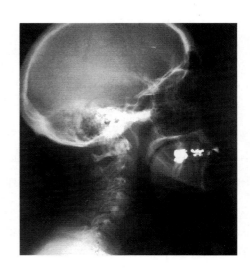

P.S. I'm including an x-ray of my skull in case things take a turn for the worse. (Please note: my mandibular third molar has a secret compartment in case you need to make a positive ID.)

-Agent S.

Subject: What Is Going On Here?
From: robcheng_jiangsutianyin@yahoo.com

ATTN: Svetlana Petrokov,

In response to your mail, we believe you should have listened to my instructions as to your transferring the money. By now you should have been able to get a safer place for your research and your life especially.

We are beginning to loose confidence in you and it seems you are not ready to get the funds transferred. The first assignment we gave was to effect the transfer and that you have not done due to one problem or the other. This is not good.

My partner and my friend, we have come a long way and I see no reason for your sudden behaviour.

Subject: Urgent Developments
From: SvetlanaPetrokov@gmail.com

Mr. Cheng, I am deeply ashamed I have let you down. I want you to know this is not in my nature. I was trained at the Department of Weaponry to complete a mission no matter what the outcome. In fact, I once walked through a building burning with nitrobenzene just to retrieve Brezhnev's favorite fur hat. This is why my body hair is now synthetic.

I am sorry for this inconvenience, but I must stress how dangerous my situation is. Agent Y followed me on my train to Minsk, so I was forced to take a detour to London. I felt I would be safe in the confines of the company headquarters. In fact, I am at The Newton House on New Bond Street right now, but the woman who answered the door has never heard of Jiangsu Tianyin Chemical Company. Mr. Cheng, how can this be?

Please sir, it is imperative that I see you. I am carrying a vile of Apetheron-X in my coat and I need to get it to you for safekeeping. The mixture is unstable and if I cannot get it to its proper temperature I'm afraid it will begin to separate. Then all my years of research will be lost and we'll be in danger of mass revolution. As a life-long Chinaman I'm sure you can appreciate this dilemma.

Meet me down the street at Wigmore Hall and make sure you are not followed. You'll know you're in the correct location when you hear Viktoria Mullova playing an octet in F major. (Boris and I will be on the front steps waiting for you. He'll be wearing a Busby and I'll be in a red wig.) Mr. Cheng, the safety of the world lies in your hands.

Your faithful partner and patriot - Agent S.

Subject: Disapointment
From: robcheng_jiangsutianyin@yahoo.com

ATTN: Dr. Svetlana Petrokov,

I am sending you this mail from the Bahamas right now as I traveled two days ago for an opening of a regional office. And again, I and my colleagues are beginning to wonder what kind of a representative you are? You are beginning to get us all scared of the fact that you are always being followed by this Agent Y or whatever.

Your personal problems should not come first before the company's responsibilities. You were not like this the first time I contacted you.

I sincerely think that at this juncture I will have to terminate your appointment and look for another person who is capable and ready to get the funds transferred so that we can commence the setting up of our regional office in Russia.

We hope that you get your problem solved and probably live a life of freedom.

Sincerely,

Mr. Robert H. Cheng

Subject: **PLEASE HELP!!!!!!!!!!**
From: SvetlanaPetrokov@gmail.com

Mr. Cheng, **CAN'T YOU SEE I AM IN GREAT DANGER?** I don't care that you're in the Bahamas right now. I need you to stop sipping tropical elixirs out of coconuts and get to London to assist me as soon as possible! If this vial of Apetheron melts, I'm afraid it will be no one's fault but your own!

I slept on the steps of The Newton House because I was unable to get a hotel room at such short notice. I am now terribly hunched over and Boris is getting testy with the pigeons. I didn't want it to come to this, but I'm afraid Agent Y may have sprinkled thallium poison in my shoes on the sleeper car to Minsk. Not only have my fingernails turned blue but the last remnants of my hair have fallen out. And Boris, who has always been robust, is patchy and vomiting Shephard's Pie all over the cobblestones.

PLEASE, I BEG YOU. YOU MUST GET ON A PLANE TO LONDON AT ONCE SO I CAN RECEIVE THE ANTIDOTE BEFORE IT'S TOO LATE!
Surely you have a dose of Prussian Blue at the company headquarters. It's the only thing that will save me now. As a loyal employee and daughter of the Republic you must come to my rescue. I'm afraid I only have 36 hours before my large intestine liquefies all over New Bond Street!

P.S Agent Y has followed me here to London. I took this snapshot of him with my ballpoint surveillance pen. Be careful of this man Mr. Cheng, his trench coat is made out of pure uranium.

Your loyal servant,

-Dr. S

Subject: You Are Acting Like A Crazy Person
From: robcheng_jiangsutianyin@yahoo.com

ATTN: Dr. Svetlana,

You still do not get it. I am a very busy man and I will not be in the UK till a weeks time because I am leaving Bahamas for Singapore for an important meeting. This was not part of what I asked you to do. You are becoming a real problem and I wonder if you have always been like this.

All I wanted was a partner to help me set up a regional office in Russia and now you are giving me headache. Thus, I am sending a mail to the bank right away to send the company's funds back to its previous account.

Your appointment has been terminated and I do not want to hear from you again!

- Mr. Robert H. Cheng

Subject: **CAN'T YOU SEE I AM DYING???????**
From: SvetlanaPetrokov@gmail.com

Mr. Cheng, how can you be so heartless? Do you have any idea how painful thallium poisoning is? I have not experienced such horrible intestinal cramps since the fentanyl poisoning I received at Vladimir Putin's last peace summit! And if that isn't bad enough, I think I'm having a bad reaction to my wig tape.

PLEASE MR. CHENG, IF YOU HAVE ANY ORGAN RESEMBLING A HEART, YOU WILL COME TO THE STEPS OF THE NEWTON HOUSE AND SAVE ME! Otherwise, bury my body next to my dear husband at 32 Alexanderplatz next to Collective Farm 100038625986. At last, his lonely, rotting corpse will have some company.

Good luck quelling your mobs of unruly revolutionaries Mr. Cheng. I hope you know you've made Chairman Mao very unhappy.

- Dr. Petrokov

Subject: Do As I Have Instructed
From: robcheng_jiangsutianyin@yahoo.com

ATTN: Dr. Svetlana Petrokov,

You have insulted my personality by saying "IF I HAVE ANY ORGAN RESEMBLING A HEART." Anyway, I can not come to London right now, not until I am done with my assignment. But I can help send you "A DOSE OF PRUSSIAN BLUE" to save the situation.

Thus, I will ask the delivery officer Mr. Kasper Gabriel of TNT Courier UK to deliver it to you as it is in the headquaters in China. You have to send him **$500.00** to enable him to get it to you in time.

I will try and see you in 5 days. Then I will give back the money you are sending him and probably get you a safe place where you can get your ass together.

- Mr. Robert H. Cheng

Subject: Did You Say Blue Donkeys?
From: SvetlanaPetrokov@gmail.com

Mr. Cheng, I think my feet have fallen off....I can't seem to find them. The woman who sweeps the steps of The Newton House keeps trying to shoo me away and she insists she's never heard of you. Why does she have three legs and no eyes? I asked if she knew Sergi from the Chernobyl plant, but she just keeps hitting me with her broom!

Please help me sir, I don't feel so good. My ears are bleeding and my fingernails came off in a rainstorm. Tell Mr. Gabriel to meet me here with the antidote, I'll give him everything I've got, including the secret compound.

Please hurry, I don't think I can hold on much longer...

- S

Subject: **GOODBYE FRIEND...**
From: SvetlanaPetrokov@gmail.com

Mr. Cheng, I just gave Mr. Gabriel all of my money, but when I asked him about the Prussian Blue he just laughed and ran off. I was able to photograph him with my spy pen, but now I'm beginning to wonder if it was Mr. Gabriel at all.

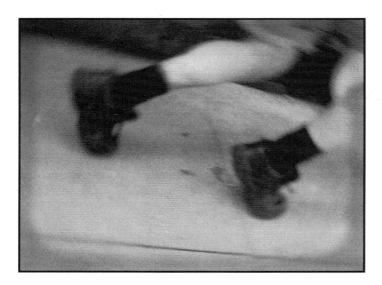

Does this agent of yours have spiked hair and a uniform advertising a "Sex Pistol"?

Not to worry, I'm afraid it is too late for me anyway. Boris is dead and my left bronchial chamber has just collapsed.

P.S. Please, do one thing for me. Call the Hotel Sovietski and make sure the chimps are ok. If they go too long without nourishment they'll eat the wall paper and wheat paste makes them jumpy.

Yours eternally,

The late Svetlana Petrokov - Chemist, Patriot, and Daughter of The Republic

---

Chapter 2.

Fudgey Carmichael

Subject: **Fudgey Carmichael**
(Future Business Partner, Former Child Star)

Con Men: **Miss Joy Johnson**
(University Student, African Heiress)
Barrister James Coullibaly
(Bank Attorney)

Attempted Swindle: $1,550

Subject: From Miss Joy Johnson
From: mailto:joy_jj3@yahoo.com

Hello Dear,

With profound respect and humble submission, I beg to state the following few lines for your kind consideration. I must confess that it is with great hopes, joy and enthusiasm that I write you this mail which I believe by faith must surely find you in good condition of health.

My name is Miss Joy Johnson. I am the only daughter of my late parents Mr. and Mrs Koffi D. Johnson. My father was a highly reputable business magnet who operated in the capital of Ivory Coast during his days.

It is sad to say that he passed away mysteriously in France during one of his business trips on the 12th September 2004. His sudden death was suspected to have been masterminded by an uncle of mine who travelled with him at that time, but only God knows the truth.

Before his death, he informed me he has the sum of **Five Million, Seven Hundred thousand United State Dollars** (USD$5,700,000.00) he deposited in a private bank here in Abidjan Cote D'Ivoire. He told me that he deposited the money in my name and also gave me all the necessary legal documents regarding this deposit. I am just 23 years old and a university undergraduate and really don't know what to do.

Now I want an honest and GOD FEARING partner overseas who I can transfer this money to. After the transaction I will come and reside permanently in your country. This is because I have suffered a lot of set backs as a result of political crisis and the death of my father brought sorrow to my life. I want to invest the fund under your care because I am ignorant of the business world.

I am in a sincere desire of your humble assistance in this regard. Now permit me to ask these few questions:

1. Can you honestly help me from your heart?

2. Can I completely trust you?

3. What percentage of the total amount in question will be good for you after the fund has been transfeered to your account and I come over to meet you?

Please consider this and get back to me as soon as possible. Immediately when I confirm your willingness, I will send to you my picture and inform you of more details.

- Miss Joy Johnson

Subject: Hi There…
From: FudgeCar50@gmail.com

Dear Joy,

It sounds like you've had some tough times, but maybe I can help. Believe me, I know all about being down and out. Can you tell me a little more about yourself?

- Fudgey Carmichael

Subject: From Joy
From: mailto:joy_jj3@yahoo.com

Dear Fudgey,

I recieved your mail response and I must not delay to tell you that I am very glad for your kind acceptance to help me out of this dilemma. I believe that my contact with you is by God's divine grace.

Please Mr. Fudgey, I want you to know that I have suffered so much down here with nobody helping me or taking care of me. The death of my father has made me go through many untold hardships. I have being praying and asking God to lead me to a trust worthied person who will honestly help me to get this money transfered into his country and I will fly to meet him for investment purposes.

I have run out of my home and I am now living hidden in a local guest house for the safety of my life. I pray that those enemies that killed my father will not kill me too.

I will like you to send me your picture and your direct telephone number for easy communication. As soon as I hear from you, I will give you more details involving this matter.

Attached below is my picture for your view. I wait to hear from you soonest.

With love and every
good wish from,

Joy Johnson

Subject: Hi Again…
From: FudgeCar50@gmail.com

Dear Joy,

You are a *VERY* beautiful woman and I want to thank you for sharing your story. Like I said, I've been through a lot of tough times too, so I think I can relate.

Maybe I should tell you a little about myself - I'm Fudgey Carmichael, the kid from that 1970's TV show "Peetie and McCleen." I was "Little Peetie," the one with the famous catch phrase,*"You got that right!"* I was originally discovered in New Orleans in a TV commercial for Hibernia Bank. I got the part because I could balance a role of quarters on my head while singing about interest rates. The ad was a huge hit and the next thing I knew I was in Hollywood with my own TV show. I was eight-years-old and as wealthy as a king, but don't kid yourself, child stars have it rough. The TV producers would rig me up with electrodes and every time the script called for it, the director would zap me and I'd have to yell out, *"You got that right!"* They used that line so many times I now have circular bald spots all over my chest.

I was in some other shows too, but I was never able to shake the "Little Peetie" character, so the work eventually just disappeared. As a washed up 12-year-old I went from drugs, to petty theft, to worse in no time flat. I pretty much hit rock bottom when I was arrested for snorting cat tranquilizers in a parking lot with Candace Crablake from "Wonder Girl and Wanda."

Anyway, things have been pretty difficult for me. I left Hollywood and I'm back in New Orleans working at a pie factory. But I'm not giving up, I still go to auditions. The trouble is, no one wants to hire a sitcom relic to sell their shampoo or used cars so I guess I'm in the typecast hall of fame. Oh well, what am I complaining about, I guess it's nothing like having your father murdered by your uncle, huh?

To tell you the truth, I could really use some of that money. If I got a 20% cut of this business deal I'm pretty sure I could re-establish myself in the industry. I'd love to call and talk to you about it, but I'm afraid I had to give up my phone because of a little debt problem, but feel free to write me anytime. I've included my picture, it will fit just about any frame.

P.S. Joy…I've been meaning to ask, do you have a boyfriend?

- Fudgey

Subject: Bank Director
From: mailto:joy_jj3@yahoo.com

Dear Fudgey,

I well recieved your picture and I must thank you for your kind effort so far.

After sending you this mail I will be going to the bank where my late Father deposited the money and introduce you to the bank director and tell him about my readiness with you. I will get back to you to let you know my outcome discusion.

Thanks and remain blessed - Joy

Subject: There's something I need to tell you…
From: FudgeCar50@gmail.com

Joy, I don't want to scare you off by being too forward, but I've really been thinking about you a lot lately. I read your last email over and over and I can honestly say I feel a certain "readiness" towards you too. I wonder what your hopes and dreams are and even what your favorite movie is. I would just die if it's "Breakin' 2 Electric Boogaloo" because I was *in* that movie. It was a small role, and I had to be taken to the hospital for a cerebral hemorrhage after the first scene, but my name's in the credits just the same.

Speaking of show business, I went to an audition yesterday for the TV show, *"Hey, Show Me Somethin'!"* It's the one where former TV stars have to make something useful out of a box of junk. I ended up making a wallet out of duct tape. They said it went really well, but I still haven't heard from them for a call back. Personally, I think I did a much better job than Bea Arthur. She tried to make pancakes out of a bag of cement and some rainwater. But honestly, who's going to be able to eat that?

P.S. Joy, you really need to tell me if you have a boyfriend. I don't want these feelings I have for you to be in vain.

Subject: Please Contact Bank…
From: mailto:joy_jj3@yahoo.com

Dear Fudgey,

I received your mail and I must tell you I am happy to know you are a movie star. Concerning the issue of having a boy friend, I would just like to let you know that I don't have a boy friend and that should be the least of my problems now because all of my aim is to transfer this money for my better future in your country before any other thing.

Meanwhile, I have been to the bank and I have told them about my readines with you to transfer my money into your account. The Bank Barrister gave me his full contact info and advised that you should deal directly with him.

Below is the contact of the bank

NAME: Bank Atlantic Cote D' Ivoire – CI

TELE-FAX :   0022521271444

HOT-LINE :   00225 0827313

CONTACT: BarristerJamesCoullibaly_ci@yahoo.com

ADDRESS: 470.BP RUE 7/A Abdijan Cote D'ivoire

Please Fudgey, get back to me after you have contacted him to tell me your out come discussion ok?

With love and every good wish from,

Joy

Subject: Ok…
From: FudgeCar50@gmail.com

Joy, don't worry, I'll write to the barrister today so we can get the ball rolling. I understand you don't want to be pressured. Believe me, I know what that's like. I was once forced to tape 10 episodes in three days without even being allowed to take a nap. After setting a Christmas tree on fire right in the middle of our holiday special I was considered a "reckless and uninsurable liability" and they had to cancel the whole season. So don't worry, I won't pressure you, but I may still write some love poetry. How do you feel about erotic limericks?

Yours,

Fudgey

Subject: Greetings Barrister
From: FudgeCar50@gmail.com

Mr. Coullibaly,

I'm going to be doing some business with Miss Joy Johnson and she asked that I contact you. She will be transferring money into my personal bank account for investment purposes. Please let me know what I need to do to complete this process. I'm quite fond of Joy and I think she's finally warming up to me, so I'd like to get this transfer done as quickly as possible before she changes her mind.

Many thanks,

Furgeson "Fudgey" Carmichael

Subject: Information Form To Please Fill Out
From: barristerjamescoullibaly_ci@yahoo.com

COMPAGNIE BANCAIRE DE L'ATLANTIQUE CÔTE D'IVOIRE

**470.BP Rue 7/A Abidjan Cote D'ivoire
Tél: (225) 0827 3124   Fax: 0022521271444
Télex : 22 365 Cobaci**

ATTN: FUDGEY CARMICHAEL

This is to acknoledge the receipt of your mail in regard to your local partner here (Miss Joy Johnson) whoose late father's fund was deposited in our bank here in banking company of the Atlantic Ivory Coast.

The bank recieved the email you sent concerning the transfer of the fund into your account in your country **USD $5,700,000.00** (five million, seven hundred thousand United States dollars) but before the bank will procceed for the transfer, we are requesting you to send all your details.   As soon as all these informations are received from you then it will enable us to process the documents of change of ownership into your own name.

Please supply:

**-YOUR FULL NAMES
-YOUR ACCOUNT INFORMATION
-YOUR FAX NUMBER
-YOUR TELEPHONE NUMBER
-YOUR I.D CARD OR YOUR INTERNATIONAL PASSPORT
-THE NAME OF YOUR COUNTRY**

Mr Fudgey, I must tell you that the Ministry of Finance charges the sum of **$1,550 dollars** in procuring the change of ownership certificate on your name as the new beneficiary of the fund. You are advised to send the money with this following name below through Western Union money transfer:

**NAME: BARRISTER JAMES COULLIBALY,
ADDRESS: PLOT BP 4 ABIDJAN COTE D' IVOIRE
CITY : ABIDJAN
COUNTRY: COTE D'IVOIRE**

Please, I hope you are capable to handle the money with your little partner Miss Joy? She told me that you are a good partner to her, but I will be pleased if both of you will be kind to each other when the money comes to you. Both of you should try a good investment that will favor you for the rest of your lifes.

Have a nice day and we are ready to render you the best of our services.

- Barrister James Coullibaly Esq.

Subject: I Sent The Info To The Barrister, Ok…
From: FudgeCar50@gmail.com

Joy,

I just want you to know I sent Barrister Coullibaly all the necessary information that he requested, like my address and bank account number and stuff. But it seems I owe him $1,550 for the change of ownership certificate. As soon as I figure out a way to get that much money I'll send it to him and you can meet me here in America.

Joy, I hope you don't find this too forward, but I'd really love it if you'd stay with me when you arrive. My place isn't big, but it's clean and I've got a TV. I work the night shift at Hubig's Pies so you'd have plenty of private time. And my room mate Floyd won't bother you. He works at the pie plant too, but he got his head caught in the dough hopper so he doesn't talk much anymore. And even though I have your picture blown up and placed beside my pillow, I promise I won't try anything funny.

P.S. I finally got a call back for *"Hey, Show Me Somethin'!"* They want me to make a windmill out of a picnic table and a lawn mower. I don't want to jinx anything, but I think my acting career may be looking up.

Loads of love,

Fudgey

Subject: Compliments of the Day To You…
From: mailto:joy_jj3@yahoo.com

Dear Fudgey,

We really need to hurry up so this transaction will take place quickly. Please, I will like you to always comply with the Barrister and pay him his funds, then I can fly to meet you in America for my better future.

Yes, I don't have anywhere to stay and it will be my pleasure staying with you, if you so wish. More so, I want to thank you once again for your compliment on my picture. I will also like you to send me another picture of you.

With love from,

Joy

Subject: My Portrait
From: FudgeCar50@gmail.com

Dearest Joy,

I am *so* happy you want to stay with me! I must confess, I'm having feelings for you that I've never experienced before. Even now, as I'm typing, I have a tingly sensation running down my leg. I don't want to scare you, but I think I may be falling in love.

I'm sending you another picture, just like you asked. This one was taken a few years back when I was doing a photo shoot for a friend's movie called "Man Boy

Mayhem." It was never released in America, but apparently it did quite well in Norway.

P.S. I told Floyd about you and he wants to know what kind of crust you prefer, butter or lard.

Yours forever,

Fudge

Subject: Your Picture…
From: mailto:joy_jj3@yahoo.com

Fudgey,

I recieved your mail. I wonder why you have to send me your nacked picture? I felt embarased seeing that…

- Joy

Subject: I didn't Mean To Upset You
From: FudgeCar50@gmail.com

Joy,

Are you mad? You sound mad. I'm sorry my picture embarrassed you but I just wanted you to know I'm a grown man who is fully prepared for love and not the eight-year-old everyone remembers from "Peetie and McCleen."

On another note, my friend Buck wants to start shooting "Man Boy Mayhem II" and call me crazy, but I think there's a part in there for you. How does "Shelly the girlfriend" sound? Like the first movie, it was going to be about naked poltergeists that set things on fire with their eyes, but the insurance for blow torches got too expensive, so now it's just going to be about zombies.

I know there are a lot of monster movies out there, but this one is gonna have a twist. You see in this movie the only way to beat the zombies is to eat *them* while they're trying to eat *you*. It's gonna have a pretty small budget but that doesn't mean it isn't going to be a quality picture. If the tax credits go through we're gonna get real blood and everything. And get this, if you take the role, you'll have 5 speaking parts and you'll only have to shave off half your hair!

Joy, I've been thinking, I wish you would open up to me more. I don't even know your favorite food, or your middle name, or whether or not you like Kung Fu movies. Please Joy, just tell me you're not mad at me. I don't think I could live with myself if you are.

P.S. I told Floyd not to bug you about pie crust. He gets a little funny when it comes to girls and processed fats.

Love and kisses,

Fudgey

Subject: I Look Forward Reading From You Soonest
From: mailto:joy_jj3@yahoo.com

Dear Fudgey,

I am not mad at you, but I am desperate because I am not comfortable down here. I really want the bank to transfer my money quikely into your account in America so that I can leave this country to fly and meet you, then we can have all the time to discuss any thing about the hollywood and the movies.

P.S. My favorite food is jelof rice and my middle name is Doyin. Please, I will like us to reserve all this further questions till I come over to meet you. I cant wait to see you and to rest in your arms. Meanwhile, have you sent the funds to the Barrister?

Thanks and remain blessed.

- Joy

Subject: FANTASTIC NEWS!!!!!
From: FudgeCar50@gmail.com

Dearest Joy, guess what? I've figured out the perfect way to get the money. Next week we're gonna host A HUGE, HOLLYWOOD-STYLE FUND RAISER FOR THE ZOMBIE MOVIE RIGHT HERE IN NEW ORLEANS!!!!

I told the director all about your father's millions and he thinks you should be a key player.   Once we get enough cash raised, I'll be able to pay Barrister Coullibaly's legal fees and you'll finally be able to fly here and be both a producer *and* have a starring role in the picture.

Oh Joy, I can't wait. It's gonna be a huge, star-studded extravaganza. We're gonna hold it in the back room at Hubig's Pies right next to the fruit pulverizer. A bunch of famous actors are gonna be there - Johnny Whitaker, Willie Aames, and even Randall "Tex" Cobb, the heavyweight boxer. I called Channel 6 so maybe they'll send over the Mackel twins and get us on the evening news. If they do a story about us there's no telling *how* big this thing could be!

Willie isn't sure he likes the idea of starring in a movie about eating the flesh of the undead now that he's a born-again Christian, so he may just show up dressed as "Bibleman," the character from his religious kids show.

I'm just sure the fundraiser will be a hit. We're even going to hand out novelty body parts to help sell the concept. Every investor that gives $100 or more gets a pair of rubber ears and an edible forearm. If everything goes right, we'll be up to our eyeballs in movie money, just you wait and see!

Subject: I Await To Hear About Your Plannings
From: mailto:joy_jj3@yahoo.com

Dear Fudgey,

I must say I am very happy and I hope this all takes place soonest. Please do as you promised and get the money quickly. I am hoping on you!

With love and best wishes.

Joy

Subject: The Fundraiser
From: FudgeCar50@gmail.com

Joy,

Ok, I'm not going to say the fundraiser wasn't a success, because I would never want to ruin your dreams of becoming a movie star, but we did have a few problems. For instance, I now know to never get a professional boxer drunk and expose him to a guy wearing tights. I'm pretty sure the cost of re-setting Aames' nose is gonna eat up at least $700 in our special effects budget. And it turns out Channel 6 doesn't show up for just any old news story, even if you send Travers Mackel a check for $20 and a box of fried pies.

So, the fundraiser wasn't quite the big money maker that I thought it would be. In fact, at the end of the night, we actually ended up losing money. Not only were the medical bills high, it turns out the fake zombie legs cost $399 instead of

$3.99 like I had thought. And Mr. Ramsey, my boss, is gonna dock my pay because Tex downed a fifth of gin and got naked in a vat of cherries.

But I don't want you to worry. You're my little movie star and I'm going to find a way to have this picture made. I guess I could see if Candace Crablake would give me a loan. After all, I've still got pictures of her doing the dirty Sanchez with an Arab.

Oh Joy…I hope you're not mad about the fundraiser. I want so badly to hold you in my arms and smell your ears.

- Fudgey

Subject: Please Remember Your Deadline
From: mailto:joy_jj3@yahoo.com

Fudgey,

I am not mad at you, I believe in you. I still have the same feelings for you and I can't wait to be seeing your face.

The barrister told me that Saturday (that being tomorrow) is your deadline with him. Try your possible best to fulfill your promise because I am tired of staying here alone. Please Fudgey, dont fail him. You know that he is man of his word. Please let there be no disappointment. For my life sake, lets make this fast to avoid any further delay. I think the delay now is from your side.

- Joy

Subject: The Deal With Candace….
From: FudgeCar50@gmail.com

To my greatest Joy,

You truly are a good person to believe in me the way you do and I long for the day I can caress your head and elbows. That being said, I guess it's ok to tell you what happened with Candace.

I was able to get a cheap flight to Los Angeles and as usual, I found her hanging out at Tattoo Mania on Sunset bumming smokes from tourists. When she was a kid on TV she was always known for her cute, perky face, but for a 28-year-old, she sure has a lot of extra neck skin. Anyway, I told her all about you and how you're going to finance the zombie movie and everything. It turns out I didn't even have to mention the pictures because she really wants to help us get the money. All I have to do is pitch in with this deal she's gotta do Sunday night. She said if everything goes ok, I should have a boat load of money by Monday morning. I'm not exactly sure what it involves except that I'm supposed to bring Sudafed, camp fuel and a whole bunch of Red Devil lye.

Don't worry, I'll write the barrister and tell him I need just a few more days to pay his legal fees. Maybe I can send him an autographed photo of myself to buy some time. I had some zombie headshots taken yesterday and the missing cheekbones look totally real.

Wish me luck, ok?

- Fudge

Subject: Dear Barrister….
From: FudgeCar50@gmail.com

Dear Sir,

I'm sorry to keep you waiting regarding your legal fees. I have a business opportunity that has come up and I promise I will have the money in just a few days.

P.S. I was going to send you a headshot from my upcoming movie "Man Boy Mayhem II: Return of the Zombie Eaters" but I ended up leaving them in the back of a street car on the St. Charles line. So instead, I'm sending a picture of an edible foot that we used for our fundraiser.

If you look closely at the ankle bone, you'll see it's signed by our leading man, Randal "Tex" Cobb.

Yours truly,

F. Carmichael

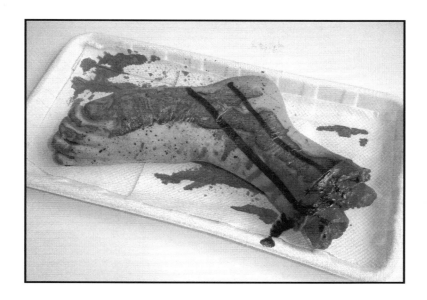

Subject: From The Office Of Barr James Coullibaly
From: barristerjamescoullibaly_ci@yahoo.com

Attention:

Bear it in mind Mr Fudgey Carmichael that my chamber is not for jokes and I am not a man that can tolerate these kinds of doings!

Mr Fudgey Carmichael, knowing you as the beneficiary receiveing the fund for Miss Joy Johnson I do not expect you to be unserious! I am waiting for the fees required to procure the documents for the transfer of the funds to your account.

Be rest assured that I have a tight schedule on my desk and I will not be able to face any bad attitude by my clients!

- Barr James Coullibaly

Subject: Regarding The Foot…
From: FudgeCar50@gmail.com

Mr. Barrister,

I didn't intend my zombie foot to be a joke, I sent it to you with the best intentions. It will be a very valuable Hollywood collectible one day. In fact, it's probably worth at least $100 on EBay right now!

Sincerely,

Fudgey Carmichael

Subject: The Candace Situation….
From: FudgeCar50@gmail.com

Dear Joy,

Don't worry about the barrister, I've got that under control. As far as the deal with Candace is concerned, I should have known it was gonna involve some kind of illegal activity, because every since she lost her sitcom she's been on a downward spiral. First it was diet pills and cocaine, but now she's into some real bad stuff. It turns out she and her roommate Spaz are cooking crystal meth in their bathtub. Last night, she sold $6,000 of it to a guy named Russo who turned around and sold it back to her for $8,000 and an alley date. Candace was too cranked up to realize she was buying back her own stuff. But the way I look at it, $2,000 should be mine for contributing materials and helping stir the ammonia pot.

So here's what I'm thinking….before I send the money to the barrister, I think we should get married. Joy, it would be wonderful! You could finally stop worrying about those bad guys coming after you in Africa because there's no way that evil uncle of yours could get you under my protection - *no way!*

What do you say Joy? How would you like to be Mrs. Fudgey Carmichael? You could send me a picture of yourself in a white dress and I could send you a picture of the ring. The whole thing could be done in just a few minutes over the Internet. Come on Joy, *just say yes…*

Love forever,

- Fudgey

Subject: I Don't Understand You!
From: mailto:joy_jj3@yahoo.com

I recieved your mail and I am in a very bad mood. Your tale to me is a vague one because I dont understand all you mean. Are you joking with me?

I want to let you know that my situation presently does not require what you are talking about. Bear it in mind Fudgey that I contacted you to help me transfer the funds of my late father for my care, not for you to marry! Even if we are to talk about that, I certainly dont beleive that this is the time because I am suffering now to settle down for my future.

If you are willing to assist me, why not come out fully and stand on it as a matured man? Kindly tell me what you intend doing at this moment because you are puting me into a frustration by your words!

- Joy

Subject: Don't Be That Way…
From: FudgeCar50@gmail.com

Joy, I'm not joking. I know marriage is a big step, but I really think you and I are made for each other. You don't have to make a decision right away. Just think how happy you'll be being married to a big-shot movie star. I promise I'll buy you anything you want, like expensive clothes, an Italian foot stool, or one of those little Mexican dogs in a sweater. Floyd even said he'd make us a special wedding pie. (Although the last time he did something like that the break in routine disoriented him and he fell into the pit extractor.)

Look, I've got one more meeting with Candace tonight and she said this deal should really bring in some serious cash. She promised Russo won't be there this time. (Thank God, his forehead scar and gigantic hands made me kinda nervous.)

- Your man Fudge

Subject: Please Answer Me…
From: mailto:joy_jj3@yahoo.com

Fudgey, I went to my pastor this morning after reading your mail. I explained everything I have been going through and your proposal to marry me. He was surprised of hearing that but he adviced me to give you his contact and tell you to get in touch with him.

He said you should send him an email with a copy of your photo so he can pray for us. Here is his contact info: PastorBright2004@yahoo.com   Phone: 00225 0651 4860

Please do not send him a naked picture of your self!

P.S. I have attached my photo again for your view.

- Joy

Subject: Hello!
From: FudgeCar50@gmail.com

Greetings Pastor Bright,

Joy Johnson gave me your email address and asked that you pray for us. We're having some real problems but maybe you can help? You see, I'm completely in love with Joy and I've asked her to marry me - but she said no! I can't tell you how heartbroken I am. I admit I'm not perfect, but I'm going to be the star of the greatest zombie movie ever made and that must count for something.

Please Pastor, could you put in a good word for me? Could you have God appear before her in a golden cloud or something? Maybe with a little cajoling He could persuade her to say yes. I can't tell you how much it would mean to me, and if it all works out, I'll invite you to the wedding. It's going to be online so you won't have to travel or starch your robe or anything.

P.S. Joy told me to send you a picture. Like I said, I'm starring in a new blockbuster movie and I just had this one taken. I'm really happy with it. It took the photographer three hours to have my lips removed!

Peace be with you.

- Fudgey Carmichael

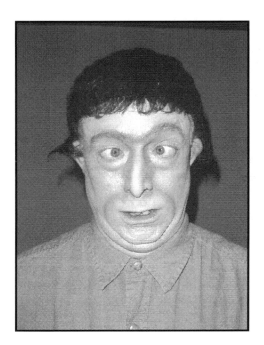

Subject: I AM PUTTING MY TRUST IN YOU, PLEASE COME TO MY AID!!!
From: mailto:joy_jj3@yahoo.com

Fudgey,

The pastor called me this morning to tell me his discaussion with you. He was suprised to see the kind of picture you sent him. He was very disapointed and complained much about it, but I let him understand the kind of person you are so after a while he promised to pray for you.

Furthermore, I want you to know that I have decided to accept your hand in marriage. That is to say that I will marry you for this reason **- I want you to try as much as you can to send the barrister his money!** Then I can come over to your country to stay with you for the rest of my life because my condition is so bad I cant even afford feeding my self.

The worst problem with me now is with the manegment of the hotel were I am staying. I have not been able to pay the hotel bills for the past 2 months. I was hoping that as soon as my money is transferred you will withdraw some and send it to me so I can settle the bill and prepare my travling documents to meet you for my better future.

As it is now, I need the some of **$300** from you to settle the bills because I have been given 4 days to pay or they will send my things out to the street. You can send the money to me JOY JOHNSON, ADRESS: BP 7 VRIDI.

Do it for me Fudgey. Please dont let shame catch me for the sake of love…

-Joy

Subject: OH MY GOD!!!!!!!
From: FudgeCar50@gmail.com

My greatest Joy,

I CAN'T BELIEVE YOU SAID YES!!!! You have made me the happiest man on Earth! I knew Pastor Bright's prayers to God would come true. So tell me, did God appear to you in a golden cloud? Did he say I was going to be a big star and you should marry me right away? Did he say anything about box office grosses for zombie movies?

I was able to exchange a few favors for a marriage license and engagement ring. I'm not going to tell you what I had to do for it because I don't want to ruin this romantic mood, but let's just say it involved something the pastor wouldn't approve of. So all you have to do now is sign this attached marriage certificate. I already had Willie and Randall sign it as witnesses and a friend of mine from the World Christianship Internet Ministry has agreed to marry us for free. I've included her credentials just so you know it's on the up and up.

Your future husband,

Mr. Fudgey Carmichael

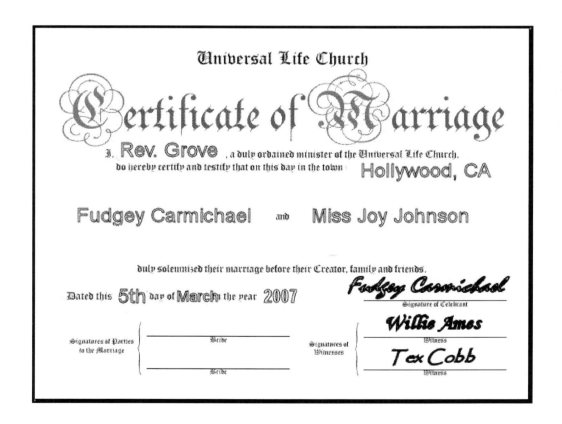

World Christianship Ministries

This credential certifies that

Rev. Diana L. Grove

has been ordained as independent Christian clergy on April 5, 2003. World Christianship authorizes this individual the authority to perform all standard Christian services including the rites of marriage and baptism.

Rev. D. E. McElroy Administrator/Bishop, Fresno, CA. 93747-8041 USA

Subject: Um…I Need To Tell You Something…
From: FudgeCar50@gmail.com

Joy, I assume you haven't gotten back to me because you've been busy shopping for a wedding dress. Well if you are, hold on, because I'm afraid I have some bad news. Joy, I just found out I can't marry you…*because I'm already married.*

I know…I'm as upset as you are. It turns out I'm married to Florine Crawford, Joan Crawford's second cousin. A few years back she got me drunk on gimlets at the premier of *Hell Comes To Frogtown*. I guess I was too intoxicated to realize The Little Chapel of Eternity in Las Vegas was for real.

The thing is, Florine just called and said she would help finance the movie - all I have to do is live with her like a real husband. I never realized how loaded she is, and you know, for a 91-year-old, she's really pretty spry. It only took her 20 minutes to get into the zombie suit.

So I guess this is goodbye Joy. I want you to know I really did love you, and every time I see a beautiful young girl eating the flesh of the dead, I'll think of you. *You got that right!*

- Fudgey Carmichael

Chapter 3.

Phebus McPhadden

Subject: **Phebus McPhadden**
   (Taxidermist, Lottery Winner)

Con Man: **David S. Roth**
   (Fiduciary Agent, Lottery Advocate)

Attempted Swindle: **$2,980**

Subject: URGENT: PLEASE OPEN TO CLAIM YOUR PRISE!!!
From: irishlotto2006@minicaragua.com.ni

P O Box 1010, 11 G Lower Dorset Street, Dublin 1, Ireland

WINNING NOTIFICATION:

Congratulations!!!! We happily announce to you the draw (#1004) of the **IRISH LOTTERY ONLINE SWEEPSTAKES INTERNATIONAL PROGRAM!**

Your e-mail address attached to ticket number:56475600545 drew the lucky number which subsequently won you the lottery in the 1st category! You have therefore been approved to claim a total sum of € **3,029,671.00 Euros.**

All participants were selected randomly from World Wide Web sites through a computer draw system extracted from over 100,000 unions, associations, and corporate bodies that are listed online. A European agent will immediately commence the process to facilitate the release of your funds as soon as you contact us.

Please be warned!!! For security reasons, you are advised to keep your winning information confidential till your claim is processed and your money remitted to you in whatever manner you deem fit. This is part of our precautionary measure to avoid double claiming and unwarranted abuse of this program.

To file for your claim, endeavour to email your **full name, email address, telephone number and photo ID** immediately.

Congratulations from me and members of staff of **THE IRISH LOTTERY.**

Yours faithfully,

DAVID S.ROTH (Esq)

Fiduciary Agent
72 Fulbourne Road, Suite 12
Walthamstow, London E174EG
Phone: +44 701 112 7404

Subject: Is It True?
From: CritterStuffer@gmail.com

Dear Mr. Roth Esq,

Top o' the morning to you! Have I really won the Irish Lottery? Boy, this comes at a good time. I'm a taxidermist by trade but my shop has been pretty hardscrabble lately due to a crack down on corn otter hunting., I barely have enough savings this month to buy limb wire.

Please let me know when you send the winnings so I don't have to fill out the bankruptcy papers. Heck, I'm so happy I'm going to go out and stuff an entire family of mud coots!

P.S. Here's my taxidermy license. It's the only photo ID I've got, but it's has all the information you'll ever need.

Yours truly,

Phebus McPhadden

Louisiana Taxidermy License

Number: 005-7756-398-BJ5

Phebus McPhadden
205 E. Bayou Rd.
Thibodaux, LA 70301

Certified Mammalian Stuffer:
Lafourche Parish, LA

"Secta Taxis Derma"   Signature: *Phebus McPhadden*

Subject: Please Pick An Option
From: dr_lyttle@yahoo.co.uk

Dear Phebus,

I am informing you that you have been officially cleared for payment by our Clearance Committee Department. You must please choose a mode of collection.

(A) Collection In Person: (Recommended) You are scheduled to be at the **OFFSHORE PAYMENT OFFICE** for the processing and claiming exercise on or before **25TH NOVEMBER.** You are advised to come with the following: 1. International passport for identification 2. Two passport photographs 3. Your first email letter of notification.

This option is recommended by the lotto management to clear any doubts and unnecessary thinking. This is because we have had a series of complaints that people are using our company name for various forms of indecent acts. So the lotto management would prefer beneficiary winners to come and verify things for themselves.

(B) Bank Transfer: An affiliated bank to the Lottery Company would be contacted and your winning would be wired directly to your personal bank account in your location.

Endeavor to contact me immediately. Good luck and congratulations once again.

- DAVID S.ROTH (Esq) - Fiduciary Agent

Subject: I Will Need A Bank Transfer
From: CritterStuffer@gmail.com

Dear Mr. Roth,

As much as I would love to go to Ireland to pick up my winnings, I'm afraid I can't leave the shop. The big Thanksgiving chipmunk season is starting and it's one of the most lucrative times for a taxidermist. Folks start calling me weeks in advance wanting their chipmunks stuffed and placed in festive poses. Last year I did a whole nativity scene with the Virgin Mary swaddling the baby Jesus. I used woodchucks for the wise men and a groundhog for Joseph, and boy was it a hit. So I guess the best thing for me would be to get one of those bank transfers.

By the way, it would be an honor to donate one of my stuffed animals to the Irish Lottery. How about a Three-Ringed Cow Elk? They're striking in an office lobby.

Yours,

Phebus

Subject: From Solicitor Roth
From: dr_lyttle@yahoo.co.uk

Phebus,

Note that your account has been opened but not active.   The funds have been credited into it but will not be accessible to you until the bank is able to verify your ACCESS CODE. This activation will only be done as soon as you have paid the necessary fee below.

Break Down Of Fees For The Activation Of Account:

Account opening fee = 1,000
Attorney legal fee   = 540
Total   =   1,540 Pounds Sterling (US $2,980)

The procedure for a direct bank wire transfer is very easy. Here are the recipient account details. You should scan or mail me a copy of the transfer receipt for the direct bank wire transfer for the payment of the mandatory fee below.

BANK WIRE TRANSFER ACCOUNT INFORMATION:

Sort code: 074456   **Acc number:** 00831218
Iban: gb17naia07011600831218   **bic:**   midl gb22
Address: # 4 Station Parade, Barking, Essex, IG 11 8 DP, England
Account name: EVBOUMWAN ISOKEN   **Bank name:**   NATIONWIDE

I await your immediate response.

DAVID S. ROTH (Esq)

Subject: Access Code Fee
From: CritterStuffer@gmail.com

Dear Solicitor Roth,

Before I pay the access code fee I'm going to have to organize my finances a bit here at the shop. I hope you understand $2,980 is a heck of a lot of money and I haven't stuffed any big game in while. I've mostly been doing small jobs like this

Wooly Pond Warbler. Believe me, it was no small task, it took me three hours just to varnish the feet!

Please be patient with me, I'll get that money to you just as soon as I can.

Yours truly,

Phebus McPhadden

Subject: Hurry
From: dr_lyttle@yahoo.co.uk

McPhadden,

How are you? Endeavour to make the payment as promised so that I can start the endorsement and validation of your funds transfer processes at the Bank. Please hurry as I must get back to my work properly. I await your payment details soon.

- DAVID S. ROTH (Esq)

Subject: Good News!
From: CritterStuffer@gmail.com

Mr. Roth,

I was a little worried I wouldn't have enough cash for the access code, but I just got a job order yesterday so there shouldn't be any problem. A buddy of mine met a big game hunter in Australia and told him what a great job I do with crepuscular quadrupeds, so this fellow has commissioned me to stuff a whole family of wombats for him. To tell you the truth, I've never seen a wombat before, but I've heard they look a little bit like a muskrat combined with a swamp pig. Anyway, after these little fellas arrive via air mail I should have the proper funds, no problem.

I sure hope deer eyes fit in a wombat socket…

- Phebus

Subject: I'm Still Waiting
From: dr_lyttle@yahoo.co.uk

McPhadden,

What is the position of things? Please endeavour to do as you say because I am a very busy man and I need to attend to some court cases, so it is your transfer procedures that is really taking my time.

Note that time is of the essence…the earlier the better to avoid forfeitment.

Yours Sincerely,

DAVID S. ROTH (Esq)
Solicitor and Advocate.

Subject: A Little Problem…
From: CritterStuffer@gmail.com

Mr. Roth,

Look, I won't sugar coat it, I had a close call here at the shop. I had everything set up to do the wombat job, but I got a real shock when I opened the shipping crate. It seems something must have gotten into the container in Australia and tried to eat its way out. (And considering the size of the gnaw marks it must have been a wallaby or a dingo or maybe one of those Tasmanian devils) So in the end, I had a whole family of endangered wombats in my shop without any ears or legs.

I was really racking my brain trying to think how to fix them, but they don't call me "Phiting Phebus" for nothing. You see, my neighbor has a mess of show corgies in her back yard, and believe it or not, they look a whole lot like wombats when you shave them down and the light is right. I'm not saying it was easy, but with a little struggle and some black dye, those ears and legs fit on just perfect. In fact, my shop would look like a petting zoo right now if there wasn't so much blood and fur everywhere.

So don't worry Mr. Roth, as soon as I get these little buggers off in the mail, I'll send the money to you fair and square.

- Phebus

Subject: Phebus You Must Take Action!!!!
From: dr_lyttle@yahoo.co.uk

Look McPhadden,

You are taking too much time! I think I have appealed to the bank on several occassions for your excuses. This time you will either finalise the access code fee or send me an email stating that you wish to forfeit your winnings! I await your urgent response.

- David S Roth

Subject: Ok Look, I Got Big Trouble Here
From: CritterStuffer@gmail.com

Mr. Roth,

There's no reason to lie, so I'll just tell you why I haven't sent the money. Like I said, I stuffed the wombats and sent them off to Rorey Ramsby, the Australian hunter, but apparently they didn't get through customs too good. Security agents opened the case in Brisbane and since some of the ears had come unattached, it took them a while to identify them as wombats. But sure enough, they still reported them as "illegal specimens of an endangered species." And if that isn't trouble enough, my neighbor found out it was me who swiped her show dogs. So now I've got an international warrant for my arrest AND the local police after me!

Is there any way you could just give me some of the lottery money in advance without paying the access code fee? In fact, why don't you just take out a percentage and keep it for yourself?

Please Mr. Roth, I'm in a lot of trouble here, ya gotta help me out.

Phebus

Subject: This Is Impossible
From: dr_lyttle@yahoo.co.uk

Dear Phebus,

There is a hard-cover insurance policy on your fund which makes it impossible for the bank to deduct your administrative charges. Also, you should kindly note that the fee is not just for the bank alone but for "I" the accredited attorney in charge of all endorsements.

Phebus, the bank is guaranteed 5% of any unclaimed winnings, but you and I would be left with nothing. *Is that what you want?*

It is your decision. Let me know what you will be able to raise in the next couple of days so I can put in a word for you at the bank.

Yours Sincerely,

DAVID S. ROTH (Esq)

Subject: PLEASE!!!!
From: CritterStuffer@gmail.com

Look Mr. Roth, I am going to be arrested for trafficking an endangered species! Please, you gotta help me, I can't sleep and my gut is going all funny. *Do you know what it's like to take the ears off a perfectly good show dog?!*

If I don't get $12,000 in the next three days I'm going to prison. That's right PRISON! And I don't think the boys in cell block H will care too much that I was supposed to get 3,029,679 million from the Irish lottery!

Please Mr. Roth, you've got to advance me some money. For the love of God man, do it for the little animals…

Subject: Urgent
From: dr_lyttle@yahoo.co.uk

Phebbus, at this time, I am sorry there is nothing I can do. If you wish to forfeit your winnings to the Bank, then send me an email stating that.

-David Roth ESQ.

Subject: THIS IS THE END OF ME!!! DO YOU HEAR?????!!!!
From: CritterStuffer@gmail.com

Mr. Roth,

Look, I'm going to jail because of you. Don't you have any kindness in your heart??? Do you know what it's like to tell a grown woman her dogs are now part wombat? Do you know what it's like to dispose of 6 little sparkle collars with heart-shaped name tags?

I'm finished Mr. Roth…and you know what else - I HATE THE IRISH! So why don't you just take your stupid stacks of filthy Irish money and shove 'em up your nose hole!

Phebus!

Subject: Calm Down
From: dr_lyttle@yahoo.co.uk

Phebus, you won't go to jail as you are saying. How much can you raise right now? I will see what I can do to help you finalise the charges for the access code fee. - DAVID S. ROTH (Esq)

Subject: MMNNAAAAAAHH!!
From: CritterStuffer@gmail.com

Well, considering I owe the U.S. customs department $12,000 I guess that means I can raise NO MONEY FOR THE ACCESS CODE FEE!

In fact, if you could see to it that I get a cash advance from the Irish people maybe I won't have my taxidermy shop taken over by a bunch of blond guys wearing bullet-proof vests!

Oh I've seen them Mr. Roth, they have stun guns and everything. They would not be deterred by a little man from Thibodaux with some sawdust and a box of lizard eyes.

Please, for the love of the blarney stone, you gotta help me!

- Phebus

Subject: Try To Get Something Together Ok…
From: dr_lyttle@yahoo.co.uk

Phebus,

There is no way they can grant your request without a part payment for your access code fee. Try to raise something, even if I must help by adding to it.

DAVID S. ROTH (Esq)

Subject: Oh, Ok…
From: CritterStuffer@gmail.com

Dear Mr. Roth,

I'm sorry I lost my temper, but the law is coming down hard on me. They're going to get a search warrant for the shop and I've got some real bad stuff in here. Honestly, I don't know what I'll do if I'm found out.

You see, a while back I started experimenting with a new taxidermy procedure called plastination. It's kind of a tricky process that involves draining bodily fluids then replacing them with liquid rubber. It's a real big business in China and a fella can make a good buck plastinating humans for the museum market. So right now I've got a few old folks that I swiped from the retirement home preserved in my back room. (They didn't put up much of a fuss. They look pretty content actually, kind of like they just got back from a vacation in Cedar Rapids.) But let's face it, I'm pretty sure this is illegal in just about any county, so now what am I going to do?

All I have left is 20 dollars, so I guess I'll send that along and you can spot me the rest, just like you said. Then as soon as the Irish money comes, I'll pay off the Department of Fish and Wildlife and I'll be in the clear.

P.S. Just to show you how grateful I am, I'm gonna send you this Triple-Breasted Swamp Beaver. It's real rare. You can use it as a fanciful book end if you like.

Thank you so much,
I will never forget this.

- Phebus

Subject: This Is Unexceptable!
From: dr_lyttle@yahoo.co.uk

Dear Phebus,

You were asked to pay the sum of US $2,980 and you are coming up with $20? **CAN'T YOU SEE THAT THAT IS NOT A PASSMARK FOR THE ACCESS CODE FEE?!**

Please try and raise something good otherwise you will forfeit the funds!

- DAVID S. ROTH (Esq)

Subject: Ok, Here's My Offer
From: CritterStuffer@gmail.com

Look, how about if I send you $100 and a mounted bass? It's real nice. You could hang it on the wall of your office, or use it as a gift for Secret Santa.

Please Mr. Roth, it's all I have. I'm telling you, the Department of Fish and Wildlife are not a nice bunch...I've heard they have access to "implements."

- Phebus

Subject: Assistance
From: dr_lyttle@yahoo.co.uk

Phebus,

I am trying to raise money to assist you to settle the bank adminstrative charges, but you are not helping matters. I will assist you with the sum of US $800 if you can borrow money to pay the rest.

That means I expect you to have come up with at least $2,000 so the bank can release your funds transfer documents. I await to hear from you urgently.

- DAVID S. ROTH (Esq)

Subject: Dear God, Thank You So Much!
From: CritterStuffer@gmail.com

Mr. Roth,

I want to thank you from the bottom of my heart! Please send the $800 to me here in Louisiana, then I can pay off the game warden and be in the clear.

P.S. I had to stash the plastinated bodies out in the sugar field in case they slap me with a search warrant. I sure hope we don't get another warm spell – that's when the wild pigs get frisky. Just look what they did to my Escort!

Your friend,

Phebus

Subject: Mistunderstanding
From: dr_lyttle@yahoo.co.uk

Phebus, I never said I would send you $800, rather I will add it to the remaining funds you are going to send the Bank!!!! I EXPECT YOU TO GET THIS DONE URGENTLY!

DAVID S. ROTH (Esq)

Subject: There's Always a Silver Lining
From: CritterStuffer@gmail.com

Mr. Roth,

I can hardly believe it but I've had a very interesting turn of events. It seems that after a little clandestine solicitation I found a fellow from Germany who wants to purchase my plastinated bodies for his traveling museum show, and boy is he willing to pay! He's particularly interested in my "Man Riding a 5 Point Buck." (And why wouldn't he? It's one of my finest specimens. I included a Stetson hat and everything.)

Mr. Roth, I realize none of this would have happened if it hadn't been for you. So as a token of my appreciation, I've decided to send you a plastinated wombat in full pounce position. It's gotta be worth a fortune considering it's endangered and all. (And just so you know, those arms are fully movable, that's a McPhadden promise.)

Before I can send it, you need to sign a Department of Wildlife customs form. As you can see, I already filled out all of the details and paid for shipping. I'll send you the access code fee as soon as you send the form back.

It's funny how things turn out isn't it? Just last week I thought I was going to jail for theft and possible manslaughter, and now I'm rolling in both German AND Irish dough. On top of that, I just got an order to stuff a whole herd of Mississippi Jumping Weasels. I guess sometimes you just get lucky, huh?

(Let me know if you'd like me to include a basket of freeze-dried kittens. They make a real nice table setting come Easter.)

Your friend from the bayou.

Phebus McPhadden

Customs Claim Form

This form certifies the listed beneficiary as soul owner of items claimed. Please sign certificate prior to collection

Account No. #33976BG749PH7   **Transport Code** # 776AGF 43

Sender's Name Phebus Patrick Shamus O'Rorey O'Fester McPhadden

Sender's Address 205 E. Bayou Rd. Thibodaux, LA U.S.A

Receiver's Phone/Fax Number 44- 701- 112- 7404

Receiver's Name David S. Roth Esq.

Receiver's Address 72 Fulbourne Rd. Ste. 12 Walthamstow, London, UK E174EG

Item Size/Weight 192 pounds, 16 cubic feet

Item Description Australian Wombat – Rubberized

Estimated Value $ 3,000 USD   **Insurance** None

Code Spec. Small Mammalian Quadruped in Full Pounce Position

Shipping Charge $ 450 USD   PAID

Receiver's Signature / Date

....

Note: Signature of receipt of goods is required prior to delivery

Chapter 4.

Demetrius Chilblain

Subject: <u>**Demetrius Chilblain III**</u>
(Metaphysical Accountant, Job Applicant)

Con Men: <u>**Normis Investment Consultants**</u>
(International Consultancy Firm
Hiring U.S Expatriates)

<u>**Barrister Guild Hall**</u>   (Attorney "on duty")

Attempted Swindle: <u>**$661.16 and Possible Identity Theft**</u>

Subject: NICE JOB VACANCY
From: normisconsultants@uk2.net

Dear Employee,

Normis Investment Consultants, established in 1995, is an international consulting firm specializing in **WORLD WIDE PROJECT FUNDING** in the private and government sector. As a **PROJECT FUNDING LOAN SYNDICATION HOUSE** and **FINANCIAL ADVISOR** we act as a bridge between borrowers and financial institutions while negotiating deal components.

Normis Investment Consultants (NIC) has an immediate employment opportunity. NIC intends to invite experienced individuals/expatriates capable of rendering expertise services in various fields of **Finance Managemant, Banking and Finance Accountancy, etc.**

ENTITLEMENT: A very attractive salary paid in US $, Sterling or Euros depending on employee home country and currency preference.

SALARY INDICATION: US $15,400.00 – USD $25, 000.00 per month
depending upon experience and field of specialization. Interested candidates are to email resume and details of experience to our recruitment office below.

OUR MISSION: To give glory to God and provide to humanity the benefits derivable through commodity trading to alleviate and enhance the condition of the poor.

HOW TO APPLY:

Send your resume to: normisconsultants@uk2.net
Phone: +447024065175 Fax:+44 (1) 7602807795

Recruitment Office
Normis Investment Consultants (NIC)
45 Woolwich New Road Woolwich, London SE186NU, UK

We look forward to hearing from you soonest.

NORMIS INVESTMENT CONSULTANTS

Subject: Resume For The Job Vacancy
From: DemetriusTheThird@gmail.com

Dear Sirs at Normis,

I'm intrigued by your offer and I'm very interested in entering the overseas job market. Before viewing my resume, let me tell you a bit about myself. I am a direct descendant of my grandfather, Demetrius Chilblain Senior, who established *The Metaphysical Accountancy Group* in Columbus Ohio back in 1892. He was the first American to intermingle existential philosophy with taxes and asset management. I have followed in his footsteps quite well, but it is my goal to expand my horizons and branch out of metaphysical numerical conception and into the world of tangible receipt notation. I am a highly motivated, loyal worker and I'm confident I would be a valuable asset to Normis Investments.

(Please note: I recently completed a seminar in "Negotiating Deal Components" with an emphasis in "Coercion and Effective Contract Misplacement.")

Yours sincerely,

Demetrius Chilblain

Resume
Demetrius Chilblain III

449 Hoodwink Ct.
Hopewell, OH 43746 U.S.A
614-239-****

Summary: A detail-oriented Asset Accountancy Expert who specializes in relative gross margins and variable profit rumination. Major skills include theoretical numerical contemplation, objective incremental equities and conceptualizing the relativity of balance sheets. A seasoned, reliable employee with abilities to multi-task, complete projects and operate multiple calculators ambidextrously.

Education: Hopewell College for Men (attended 1968-1974). Majored in Theoretical Long Division with an emphasis in Definitive Multiplication. Minored in The Number 9. Dissertation completed 6/2/74 – "If You Carry The Three, What Will The Two Think?"

Employment:

1996-Present: **Chilblain, Keloid and Boil Accounting Firm**
Head Accountancy Manager
Responsibilities: Tax Askirtment, Creative Equity Burial and Bankruptcy Protection

1985-1996: **The Barry Dilldrop House of Assets**
Assistant Asset Manager and Gross Margin Specialist
Responsibilities: Management of assets of greater and lesser margins

1984-1985: **The Gonzales Brothers Circus**
Head Accountant
Responsibilities: General accountancy, book keeping, trapeze calibration

1977-1984: **Demetrius Chilblain Metaphysical Accounting and Phrenology Center**
Junior Accountant and Assistant Cranial Mapper
Responsibilities: Theoretical existential accounting, accurately recording skull measurements, occasional dusting

1975-1977: **Peace Corp of America – Accountancy Division**
Abacus Repairman: Namibia
Responsibilities: Repairing mathematical systems and light peacekeeping

References:

       Harry Keloid (Keloid and Shingles Accounting 614-822-****)

       Barry Dilldrop (Dilldrop "The Numbers Man" 614-224-****)

       Ernesto "El Loco Gato" Gonzales (The Gonzales Brothers Circus, corner of Main St. and I-35)

Subject: Your Qualification Is Found Suitable
From: normisconsultants@uk2.net

Dear Demetrius Chilblain,

With reference to your application for employment in pursuant to the service contract, we hereby notify you that your qualification was found suitable for the requirements of Normis Investment Consultants.

Hereinafter, you shall be required to serve as Master onboard **MV Hamm** for the fulfillments and requirements Normis Investment Consultants in United Kingdom.

Your salary shall be **US$/GBP£ 15,400.00 per month** and your leave rotation shall be 3 months on and 4 weeks off. You will be expected to join the vessel on the 31st of October.

Do provide us with your personal telephone number, the name of your nearest airport and a copy of your international passport, as this will enable our company representatives to process your travel documents, which includes your return flight tickets and visa.

You are now requested to contact our attorney Barr.Guild Hall (**ghallchamb@yahoo.co.uk Phone; +447031899787**)

You must cover the cost of the fee of your **Temporary Working Permit (TWP).** Then we will process and arrange your traveling documents including your visa and send you your prepaid return flight tickets to arrive at your port of joining in order to resume duties onboard the vessel. We hope you understand our position and act accordingly.

Attention: We seek to let you know that we have been trying to contact you through telephone and detail you about your Visa and air ticket, but could not get to you. Due to all the inconvines, I would like to let you know that all our contacts will still go ahead by e-mail.

Normis Consultants

Subject: Thank you very much
From: DemetriusTheThird@gmail.com

Dear Normis,

I am delighted to hear I have the job, although I have never been a master of a ship before. Frankly, I didn't know accountants were qualified to do such things.

My deepest apologies about the phone trouble, I was practicing transcendental division and I got so carried away with an elusive 9 that I forgot to plug the phone in. I hope this doesn't tarnish your opinion of me. I'm an extremely hard worker and I look forward to this opportunity to work in Woolwich. (I think that's where my socks are from and they're first rate!)

Could you please send me a bit more information on the job position? For instance, what kind of implements do you have for fiduciary incremental equities? Should I bring my own, or would they be ineffective due to the Trans-Atlantic gap? Also, my wife has asked if she can join me on board. She once won an award for her breaststroke so I can assure you she would be excellent Hamm material.

P.S. I will contact the barrister immediately regarding the fee.

-Demetrius Chilblain III

Subject: Please Send Me The Pertinent Information
From: DemetriusTheThird@gmail.com

Dear Barrister Guild Hall,

I am writing to alert you of my recent job acceptance by Normis Investment Consultants. I was informed that I will be the Master of the sea vessel MV Hamm. I understand I am to send you a work permit fee. Please let me know how much to send and the best method of payment.

Yours on the high seas,

Demetrius Chilblain III

Subject: Please Pay Processing Fee
From: ghallchamb@yahoo.co.uk

Dear Demetrius Chilblain III,

Compliments of the day! To process and arrange your working permits you have to remit this fee, which is **330 GBP** to United Kingdom. You have limited time. Make the fee payable through **Western Union Money Transfer** and send us the **Money Transfer Control Number.** Then you have to scan the payment clip and send it to me as an attachment. The payment destination should be;

Name of Receiver: Mr. Guild Hall
City of Destination: London
Country of Destination: United Kingdom

Expecting your kindest reply today.

- Guild Hall (Esq)

Subject: A Few Questions…
From: DemetriusTheThird@gmail.com

Dear Normis,

I want you to know I have contacted Barrister Guild Hall, but he has required I pay 330 pounds for the work documents. Please keep in mind, the United States hasn't used that kind of money since the days of Raymond Burr. How should I go about completing this transaction effectively?

I also have a few questions about the job opening. For instance, will there be life boats, if so, are they the rowing or the outboard-motor kind? I suffer from distended fibuels in my humerus due to an out-of-body experience gone awry so I'm afraid rowing will be out of the question.   But have no fear, that will in no way hinder my job performance as I plan to wear a life jacket at all times.

P.S. You never said if it would be ok for my wife to join me? She doesn't eat much and she's quite fond of sailors.

- Demetrius Chilblain III – Accountant, Existentialist,
  Future Sea Captain

Subject: Thank You, Please Be Notified
From: normisconsultants@uk2.net

Dear Demetrius Chilblain,

Thank you for the explaination you made about your health on the job we are offering you. We are herein letting you know that your working for Normis Investment Consultants will be on our ship section to be an accountant there and not be a captain of any type.

I know that United States use dollars and here in United Kingdom we use pounds. You have to go and change your currency at the bank to British pounds before making the payment.

It is possible for your wife to join you in United Kingdom. Do provide us a copy of your international passports and send a copy to our attorney. Am expecting your kindest reply by next week ok? No delaying.

- Normis Investment Consultants (NIC)

Subject: Wonderful News!
From: DemetriusTheThird@gmail.com

Normis,

Being an accountant I should have known I would need to exchange the money first. I must confess, my recent interest in transcendental time warps sometimes gets me confused.
I took a seminar on the subject last month with the great Dr. Charles McSnare. Afterward, I spent six days in Restoration England having tea with the Duchess of Cornwall. Needless to say, we had quite a nice conversation about crumpets and Highland tweed.

My wife was so thrilled to hear she will be able to join me on the ship, she ran out and bought a white jump suit and matching hat. Personally, I thought the eye patch was a bit much but it does go nicely with the hip boots.

I'm afraid we don't have any passports at the moment but perhaps my library card will suffice? Many thanks and God save the Queen!

- Demetrius

Hopewell Public Library Card

Patron: Demetrius Chilblain
449 Hoodwink Ct.
Hopewell, OH 43476

Number: 0054682385-B328-09

Special Privileges: Use of photocopier and electronic slide rule

Signature: *Demetrius Chilblain The Third*

Subject: Change Currency
From: ghallchamb@yahoo.co.uk

Dear Demetrius Chilblain III,

I have been waiting to hear from you. What happen? Why have I not received your payment clip up till this moment?

- Guild Hall (Esq)

Subject: My Apology…
From: DemetriusTheThird@gmail.com

Dear Sir Hall Esq.

I'm sorry I have not been in contact with you, but I am slightly worried that I have missed the deadline for the HMS Hamm. I do hope they'll hold the ship and not make me swim out to meet them at low tide. Is it possible Normis has gone off to sea without the ship's chief accountant? If so, how would they manage the log books and keep track of the rum barrels?

I know I should have sent the 330 pounds for the work permit by now, but the truth is, I was on my way to Western Union when I had a panic attack. I momentarily glanced up at the sky to spot a passing woodcock when I saw a wispy cloud formation that resembled the arms of a giant squid. The next thing I knew I was on a stretcher surrounded by stethoscopes and syncopologists at Victory Memorial.

You see, Mr. Hall, I have a pathological fear of cephalopods. Ever since I was attacked by a giant sea squid on one of my father's wave contemplation missions in the Gulf of Siam I have never been the same. Just glancing at my mottled, sucker-riddled skin makes my knees weak and my brow clammy. (Here is a photo of my forearm for your medical records.)

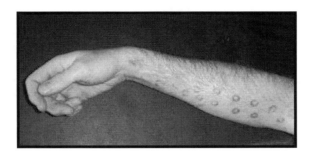

But have no fear, I am undergoing counseling with an excellent doctor who specializes in acceptance therapy for cephalophobia. He insists I remain in the house within close squid proximity until my fear has completely subsided. I am instructed to caress and speak softly to the beast at least three times a day and four on Sunday. As soon as this phase of the treatment is complete, I will then be ready to pay the work permit fee and prepare myself for the high seas.

On another note, I was wondering if it would be possible for my son to join me? He is a merchant marine and currently off duty. I'm sure his presence would be appreciated on board as he holds a full marine license in barnacle removal. He's a bit simple, but I can assure you he's a good boy.

Just to show you how entrenched he is with the sea I'm including a picture of him with his pet snapper, Jennifer.

Yours in haste,

Demetrius Chilblain III

Subject: HMS Hamm Launchings
From: normisconsultants@uk2.net

Dear Demetrius Chilblain III,

Thank you for the information. I want to let you know that I have contacted the Barrister about your issue and he has accepted my apology on your behalf.

Your launch date has been updated till 20th of this month. We hope you understand our position and act accordingly to resume duties onboard the vessel on the given date. We want to let you know that your sons arrival was approved but you have to submit your TWP to us first. **We give you three days in submitting this!!!!**

- Normis Investments

Subject: I'm Sorry About The Wait
From: DemetriusTheThird@gmail.com

Dear Normis,

I understand your urgency, but I have wonderful news - I have successfully completed squid therapy! It turns out I was completely wrong about cephalopods, they aren't the flesh-ripping, beak-nashing beasts I thought they were. In fact, I never knew they could make such loving pets. All they require is a bucket of krill and three gentle mistings a day.

On another note, my son Demetrius IV (or "Bill," as we call him) has been crafting a multi-compartment sea chest out of rare Ethiopian mahogany. This chest will have plenty of room for storing life jackets, whaling guns, sea treasure, rum, and Bill's extra leg (he lost one of his in a deck mopping incident). It is of the highest quality and quite practical for any seafaring man. In fact, we were wondering if you'd like one? If so, would you prefer a mermaid or a narwhal on the lid?

- Capt. Chilblain III

Subject: Get Back To Me Today!
From: ghallchamb@yahoo.co.uk

Dear Demetrius Chilblain III,

Please, I am a very busy man. I have received a call from Her Majesty British High Court. **We want you to know that you have to start up your work at Normis Investment Consultants by today!** All the same, why have you not remitted your TWP to enable us to complete your traveling document so you can work in United Kingdom?

I don't understand what is going on there? You told me that you have the fee to make the payment, but up till this moment you have not. If you know that you can't make it, kindly contact N.I.C head office on this issue!

The Borad of Directors at Normis Investment Consultants are not happy with you up till this moment! I want your personal phone number so we can talk like able men.

-Guild Hall (ESQ)

Subject: A Slight Issue…
From: DemetriusTheThird@gmail.com

Dear Barrister Hall Esq.

I certainly hope I'm not in trouble with Her Majesty's High Court. I know the Queen is very busy and I wouldn't want to be any bother to her. If it would smooth things out, you can tell her I'd be more than happy to prepare her taxes metaphysically. That should give her at least a 17% advantage next quarter which could easily finance another invasion of the Falklands.

On another note, I'm afraid we're in a slight pickle over Bill's leg. It seems it needs a special titanium swing flange that is only made in Switzerland. Unfortunately, it's on back order. He is the only one in the family who can drive and since he's missing a clutch foot we've been rather house bound of late. Do you think you'd be able to expedite this since you are rather chummy with the Queen?

I must stress how urgent this is. If we don't get that leg we won't be able to go out and get food, let alone the TPW money! Anything you can do will help greatly. Please, we are getting hungry.

P.S. I'm afraid I've been unable to locate the phone ever since we got our pet squid, Charlotte. She's a nervous eater and the new shag carpeting just sets her off.

-Demetrius

Subject: I Don't Need This Type Of Email From You Again!
From: ghallchamb@yahoo.co.uk

Demetrius,

WHAT KIND OF HUMAN BEING ARE YOU?!!! Listen Mr, just go to the bank and make the payment and do not to be e-mailing me back with storys everyday!

With respect to the e-mail you send to us consigning Her Majesty High Court and other things in the mail we couldn't understand, Normis Investment Consultants wish to inform you that you may have lost the job if you don't know what your doing!

I am not here to play with you, but rather do my job. If you have a problem with your self, kindly have a talk with your wife and do not be emailing me on it! I will reach Normis about this issue because **I have had too much of you!**

If you know that your not ready to make the payment of your TWP, kindly contact Normis immediately and stop emailing me some kind of story!

I am telling you this for the last time!

- Guild Hall (ESQ)

Subject: Please, Don't Be Upset…
From: DemetriusTheThird@gmail.com

Barrister Hall,

Please, I know my delays have been trouble, but you have no idea how difficult things have been. With Bill's left leg missing we are unable to leave the house and no one will bring us groceries. I have attempted transcendental hypnotherapy to make dinner appear, but it has proved unsuccessful. If we don't fix this situation soon, we shall certainly perish.

All I wanted was to be a metaphysical accountant on the high seas, but I'm afraid I have led my family to ruin. I have missed the ship's deadline, I have failed to pay the work permit fee, and I can't even get in a car to buy my family a chicken dinner. Please, is there anything you can do to help us? Our situation is dire and my mind is fading…I can't even remember how to carry a three. How can a man who studied under the great Charles McSnare have failed so miserably?

All I'm asking is for you to drop a note to the Queen and maybe send us some bread. Please, I'm beginning to feel dizzy…

Yours in rapid depletion… D.

Subject: This Is It!
From: normisconsultants@uk2.net

Att: Demetrius

You think that your family has fallen inside the well because of Normis Investment Consultants? Your wife is not there to help you, your son is sick, a squid is now the king of the house and you yourself are metaphysical? And your now seeking help from Normis? All of these are a nice story...

Now listen, we have requested your passport, we have not seen any. We requested your personal house/mobile number, we have not seen any. We have requested the address of the nearest airport, still we have not seen any of these from you. And we make your Visa/flight ticket free for you, and yet your not greatful!?

Now you want Normis Investment Consultants to come down to United States of American and clean up your family for you? And your statement, "I can't even remember how to carry a three!" "How can a man who studied under the great Charles McSnare have failed so miserably?" What is this meaning??????

Kindly write a letter to the attorney consigning this issue that you are not ready to work with us!

For the last time, that is all!

- Normis Investment Consultants (NIC)

Subject: Dear God, I'm Fading...
From: DemetriusTheThird@gmail.com

Normis,

You're right, I'm not worthy. I have absolutely no business stepping foot on the MV Hamm. I'm just a lowly accountant from Hopewell, Ohio with distended fibuels and cephalopod issues. Please know I had every intention of donning my sea boots, sharpening my decimal pencil and delving into tax askirtment on the high seas. Alas, that is not to be. I must put my dreams aside and console my wife. I'm afraid she has grown weak from eating nothing but bread crumbs and an air fern.

Sally forth merry Old England and may your conquests be great!

P.S. Please tell the barrister Bill and I handcrafted a sea chest for him. We even engraved a portrait of the royal family on the lid. (Bill got the burnishing iron a little too hot so the Duchess of Cornwall looks a bit like George Washington Carver, but other than that, it's first rate!)

Yours in metaphysical accountancy,

- Demetrius Chilblain III

Chapter 5.

Bradlowe Crumley

Subject: Bradlowe Crumley
(Coal Miner, Investor)

Con Man: Martin Mensa
(Retired African Gold Miner, Millionaire)

**Attempted Swindle: Amount Undetermined,
Possible Kidnapping and Identity Theft**

Subject: Contact Me!
From: margold212@yahoo.co.uk

Attention friend:

I am a civil servant with the government of my country, Ghana, situated in the western part of Africa. We have a gold mining company which I am the managing director.

I have worked for so many years and very soon I will be retired from service. I note those who did not plan well before retirement always end up dejected and rejected. So, I have decided to invest the little money that I have acquired over the years into something that will be profitable to me. The amount is **$15.6 million USD**. And I am prepared to part with 15% of this amount if you will assist me. The money is safely deposited with a security company in Accra-Ghana and I did not declare what was inside. If you are ready to help, please send me your full profile. For instance:

**1. Your Age
2. Type of Work
3. Telephone #
4. Passport picture**

Once you send this, I will give you the form to fill out for the security company where an account will be opened in your name after being transfered to where you choose. Also, I will be happy if you can help me to get addmission into a very nice university for my son David who will be representing me over there.

- Martin Mensa

Subject: Sounds Interesting
From: BOCrumley@gmail.com

Dear Mr. Mensa,

It's quite a coincidence you wrote to me because I'm a miner too. Heck, I've worked for Pittfield Carbon for 20 years now as a coal coupler and I've got lungs so black I must have bats hanging from my rib cage.

It sounds like mining in Africa is a little different than mining in America as far as pay goes. $15.6 million dollars is a lot of buckets of coal in this country. I haven't done the math yet but 15% seems like a pretty fair deal. I sure would like to hear more. In the mean time, I'll ask the boys down the hole about some good schooling facilities.

By the way, what does your son study? Not that it's any of my business, but how about bovine health? There's a technical college in town that's offering quite a few courses on it next semester and I hear its top notch. Here's the information about me you requested…keep in touch!

Name: Bradlowe O. Crumley
Age: 44 years old
Occupation: Coal Miner
Phone: 548-9336 (out of order due to a faulty red wire)
Passport: (I don't have one of those yet so I'm including my Pittfield ID card below)

Subject: Thank You For Your Kindest Response
From: margold212@yahoo.co.uk

Dear B. O. Crumley

Thank you very much for your prompt response to my business proposal. I appreciate the brief content of your mail, which clearly indicates your willingness to assist me in realizing this golden opportunity.

I have prayed and committed this transaction into the hands of God almighty and I strongly believe that this relationship I am establishing with you is based on trust and in benevolent spirit and will not lead to jeopardy. Rather, your utmost cooperation, sincerity and confidentiality will be given to me in course of this transaction, as it will be for posterity.

Understand that I deposited this fund in the security company using a foreign partner as the beneficiary of the consignment for security reasons. Therefore I will appreciate you to stand as my foreign partner to enable us to sign out the consignment from the security company.

This will require your presence in Accra-Ghana to sign the necessary documents that will facilitate the release of the fund. Also, your visit will afford us the opportunity to acquaint with each other, thereby dicussing possible investment in your country.

In regards to my son, he has passed secondary education with good grades. Honestly, I would like you to use part of this fund to purchase a house for us in a remote area where it will not be too costly.

As you understand, since our fate is ruled by chance, each man unknowingly, great or small, should frame life so that at some future hour fact and dreams shall meet.

Remain blessed while I anticipate your earlier response.

Yours truely,

Martin Mensa

Subject: Accra-Ghana?
From: BOCrumley@gmail.com

Mr. Mensa,

You sound like a real spiritual kinda fella. I don't know too much about otherworldly things, but one thing's for sure, I can help you out with living arrangements. In fact, I've got just the place. I have a real nice out building on the edge of my property and with a little shovel-out it could be quite cozy. I've included a picture below.

(Don't let the rotten tires and pond muck scare you. I'll put some boots on the wife and she'll give it a good once over - she's real handy with a mop.)

P.S. Ghana seems awful far away. Are there any motels, or would I have to share a hut with one of those African witch doctors?

Your friend Bradlowe

Subject: No Jokes
From: margold212@yahoo.co.uk

I want to know if you are really interested in this transaction needless of wasting our time. If not just tell me, I am giving you an opportunity to make money. It's left for you to decide, as you can take the horse to the sea but you cannot force her to drink water.

Please respond only if you are interested.

Martin

Subject: Now Don't Get All Sore Headed
From: BOCrumley@gmail.com

Look Martin,

You asked if I'm interested in your transaction - of course I'm interested! What more do I have to do to gain your trust? Don't you know it goes against the miner's code to not help a brother in need? If you need your funds dispersed, mark my word, I am a man who knows dispersal. (And try not to worry too much about the horse business. Horses are just mules without the snappy hats.)

But Martin, if we continue with this deal, you're going to have to give me more information about coming to Africa. You never told me if I'll be staying in a hotel? I'm a man of adventure, but I'm not too keen on sleeping out in the jungle with those Zulu fellows sneaking around with blow darts.

On another note, I've got some good news about the shed out back. I've got it completely cleaned out and I'm busy putting on an addition. I spot welded a few storm windows together so now you've got a real nice sun room. I had to chase out a family of raccoons that built a nest in the rafters, but after a good shake out it will be nice enough for a king.

P.S. My wife is a real worrier and she keeps insisting I bring a firearm to Africa. Is it true elephants get shifty if you approach them from behind? If so, I can always bring my Winchester field bazooka.

Your friend, same as before,

Bradlowe

Subject: Contact The Company
From: margold212@yahoo.co.uk

Dear Bradlowe,

I am telling you that you will have nothing to regret at the end of this. You coming to Ghana will give us the opportunity of knowing each other better.

You asked if there is a hotel in Africa and I am telling you that we have very good hotels here. If you really want to assist me, do not be afraid of any such thing in your mind because I am living in the capital city of Accra, not in the village. So feel free to visit, as you are planning, and I bet you will never regret it.

Now I will like you to contact the security company were the fund is deposited and introduce yourself as the real beneficiary. Please, I did not disclose what is inside the lugages as money. I just told them it is a gift owned by a "foriegn associate."

Below is the security company address. Fill out the form and send it so they will contact you and tell us what to do. Also, do not hesitate to inform me of every detail.

Hoping for the best - Martin

GLOBAL TRUST AND SECURITY COMPANY
10B CIRCLE POINT, ACCRA-GHANA
TEL: 00233-20-8972673.
EMAIL: global_9000@yahoo.co.uk

APPLICATION FOR CHANGE OF OWNERSHIP

I hereby apply to the above named company for change of ownership of consingment with deposit number xxx/pp/54/0026/01, as against the former depositors name
Mr. Martin Mensa
of NO-56 Close Road Accra-Ghana

I am applying as the foreign bussines partner to him. My particulars are as follows for the change of ownership.

Full Names:..
Addrese:..
Telephone:...
Fax..
Nationality:..
Date of Birth......................................
Your's Signature..................................

Subject: I Need To Ask You Something…
From: BOCrumley@gmail.com

Martin,

I sent the security company the form with all of my personal information, just like you asked. Don't worry, I didn't tell them the luggage is filled with money. I said it was just some old clothes that you didn't want falling into the wrong hands. (I kinda hinted it involved some "ladies undergarments with see-through panels," so I'm pretty sure they won't be asking any questions.)

Look, I don't mean to offend you, but there's something I need to ask before I go any further. One of my buddies down in the hole told me to be careful about correspondences from Africa. He saw a news report that said fellows who send emails from Ghana drug folks up, cut out their kidneys and sell them on the black market. Martin is that true, because I was born with an unusually high number of kidneys. You see, I've got 6 and I've already donated 2 of them to the Knights of Columbus!

As a friend, you gotta answer me truthfully. Do you really need my kidneys? For God's sake, there's no need to steal them when all you have to do is ask!

Your friend,

Bradlowe

Subject: WHAT?????????
From: margold212@yahoo.co.uk

Mr. Bradlowe,

WE ARE NOT CANIBATES! If you think that, you can not come to Africa! Let me know so that I can find another alternative for me to proceed!!   - Martin

Subject: Hold Up Now…
From: BOCrumley@gmail.com

Now look here Martin, I didn't mean to offend you. When you tell me you're not "canibates" what I think you mean is you're not "cannibals." Heck, I never accused you of eating a guy, I was just asking if you want my kidneys. Like I said, I've got two extra that are just taking up space.

On another note, I just signed your son up for "Rudimentary Calf Birthing 101." I think he'll like it. It's supposed to offer plenty of hands-on experience.

P.S. Say, would you like to come by the house to see the curtains my wife made for the shed? They're gingham.

- Bradlowe

Subject: Arrangements
From: margold212@yahoo.co.uk

Bradlowe, is better you come to Ghana so that we can meet in person. Please let me have your details and when you will be arraiving so that we can visit the company together and complete the modalities.

Regards,

- Martin

Subject: Africa, Here I Come!
From: BOCrumley@gmail.com

Ok Martin, I've made all the arrangements and it looks like I'll be arriving this Saturday. What's the temperature in Ghana? Should I bring a casual pant suit or would I be better off with jungle boots and netting?

P.S. My wife baked a tuna casserole for the plane trip. I sure hope they offer forks.

Your friend,

Bradlowe

Subject: Your Flight
From: margold212@yahoo.co.uk

Thanks very much for your kind of thinking by coming to Ghana. Please, I will like to have your flight schedule so that I will pick you up with my car and keep you in a nice hotel.

- Martin

Subject: Arrival Time
From: BOCrumley@gmail.com

Martin,

I will be arriving tomorrow afternoon at 3 p.m. I'll be wearing a blue double-knit suit and a white fedora. My wife found the hat in the attic. It's a little dusty, but she says it makes me look "transcontinental." Here's a picture so you'll recognize me.

P.S. Don't make a fuss about a hotel, I'd be happy to sleep right on the couch. But I should probably tell you I'm allergic to straw.

Yours,

Bradlowe

Subject: OK, I'M HERE!
From: BOCrumley@gmail.com

MARTIN WHERE ARE YOU?

I'm in the airport in Guyana, but I don't see you. Please come pick me up. Why is everyone here Spanish-looking? This doesn't seem like Africa at all. It's getting late and I don't have anywhere to stay.

A man wearing grass shoes told me I could sleep on the floor by the mens room, but quite frankly all of the *"Beware of Pickpockets and Kidnapping"* signs have me a little worried. I already ate the tuna casserole and now I'm getting hungry.

Martin, I've been waiting for you for hours. Where the heck are you?

Bradlowe

Subject: I WILL COME!!!!
From: margold212@yahoo.co.uk

Bradlowe,

Please call me now. Here is my cell phone 0208972673.

I WILL COME PICK YOU UP!

Martin

Subject: Help, This Place Is Strange…
From: BOCrumley@gmail.com

Martin,

I've been looking for you but all I see are brown people with mustaches. I spent the night here at the airport because I didn't want to miss you. It was rough, but I ended up sleeping behind a big potted palm next to the luggage carrousel.

Why doesn't my money work here? I tried buying a banana taco but the man behind the counter just laughed when I handed him a 10 dollar bill. And to make matters worse, when I tried calling you, the pay phone wouldn't accept any of my quarters. I feel like I'm trapped in a nightmare with no way out. Please come and get me friend, I'm hot and my pant suit is starting to attract flies.

P.S. You'll find me next to the curried mutton stand in concourse D.

Yours,

Bradlowe

Subject: Call Me!
From: margold212@yahoo.co.uk

Dear Bradlowe,

I came there, but I did not see you so I left. Call and tell me the possission from where you are. I will come in the next 30 minutes. Ask airport officers to show you where to change money.

Subject: Ok, I'm Standing Next To a Man With a Beard
From: BOCrumley@gmail.com

Martin,

I'm afraid I'm in a bit of trouble here, but not to worry, a very nice man in a white suit gave me some money to buy a fried beef tongue, so I'm not as hungry as I was this morning.

But here's the thing - he says that I'm in GUYANA and not GHANA, which is apparently someplace completely different. Anyway, do you think you could swing by and pick me up? I'm sure it won't be too much trouble. It's probably right on the way to the grocery store.

P.S. I'm standing next to a man who looks like Colonel Sanders except he has gold teeth and a monkey.

Your friend Bradlowe

Subject: Attn Bradlowe
From: margold212@yahoo.co.uk

I am not crazy ok. I can see that you are suffering from monopurse. I am so sorry. Please die in peace…

Subject: Not To Worry, Everything Is OK!
From: BOCrumley@gmail.com

Look Martin,

There's no reason to be sore. I know we had a bit of a screw up, but it all turned out ok. The man with the gold teeth said he would drive me to Ghana if I would just give him my hat and some money to pay for his son's medication. He said it wouldn't be more than about $800 and that's probably much less than a plane ticket if you think about it.

I can assure you I'm not "suffering from monopurse," whatever that means. On the contrary - I'm as healthy as a horse! So stop fretting around so much and put a roast on the fire. If everything goes ok, I should be there in a day or two.

P.S. The man with the gold teeth seemed real interested in my kidneys. You see Martin, you don't have to be a "cannibal" to take an interest in one of God's miracles.

- Bradlowe

Subject: Gold Dust For Sale!
From: margold212@yahoo.co.uk

ALLIED SURVEY MINING CO.LTD

**37 TOP ROAD MAKOLA
ACCRA GHANA
PHONE:+233208972673.**

Dear Friend,

I would like to introduce our company ALLIED SURVEY MINING CO.LTD. We are miners of diamond gems, industrial stones, solid gold and dredgers of alluvial gold dust. Our company is willing and ready to sell between 100-500 kgs of gold dust.

QUANTITY......500 KGS
PURITY...........91.67 PERCENT CLEAN
QUALITY.........22+ KARATS.

Thank you for your anticipated co-operation. I remain to hear from you soonest.

Regards,

Martin Mensa

Subject: Gold Dust?
From: BOCrumley20@aol.com

Martin?

Is that you? Did you get a new job? I went with the man with the big shiny teeth and now I don't feel so good. We drove and drove and when we arrived at his village I was fed a bowl of green pudding and that's all I remember. Now I have a bandage on my side and I keep coughing up blood. And why does this old woman keep handing me bags of ice?

Martin, what is alluvial gold dust? Will it get me out of here? If I buy 500 kgs will you let me stay with you? I have to tell you, I don't like it here. The monkeys are mean and the children keep poking me with sugar beets.

You have to come and get me. I have your son's class schedule in my suitcase. I signed him up for "Parasitic Elimination of The Third Stomach" but they said I need your signature. Please hurry Martin, they say it fills up fast…

Your friend,

Bradlowe

Chapter 6.

Dr. Bifida Hendrix M.D.

Subject: <u>Dr. Bifida Hendrix M.D.</u>
(Landlord, Doctor of the Spine)

Con Man: <u>Hanna Jones</u> (Health Care Worker, Potential Tenant of the Gentle Movements Spine Care Center)

Attempted Swindle: <u>$2,600</u>

Apartment For Rent

Nice room available with view of large oak tree.
Seeking quiet, peaceful tenant who enjoys
music, reading and polite conversation.
Serious inquiries only.
Contact BifidaHendrixMD@gmail.com

Subject: Apartment For Rental
From: hanna_jones002@yahoo.com

Hello,

My name is Hanna Jones, I am writing just to confirm if you still have room for rent.

Here is all I can say about my self for now. I am a 28 years old female and I work full time Monday through Friday. I was born in UK WOOD GREEN but I was brought up in England. I am presently in LAGOS STATE IN WEST AFRICA and I will be moving to the States to fully start a new life. There I will get my own business after 8 years of service in the Mild May Health Company in Africa where I am one of the perfect workers of the hospital. What we do is give medicine and advice to those with the positives of disease. Now our next contract is in the States and I saw your ad that you have a room to rent. I will like you to email me back if you think I will be a good roomie to you.

I am a very outgoing person and fun to be with. I do play the organ and piano and I do have BOTH piano and organ here at my house. I am not a drinker and I don't smoke and I don't do drugs. I am not really a sports person, BUT I do love Hockey Games.

I will be staying in your apartment for A YEAR or more and I will be arriving as soon as possible. Please I will like to have answers to the following questions below:

1) I will like to have the description of the room, size, and the equipments in there.

2) I will like to have the rent fee per month plus the utilities AND YUR MODE OF PAYMENT ???

3) I will like to know if there is any garage or parking space cos I will have my own car.

4) I will also be coming with some of my furniture, that is if the room is not funished, like a bed, shoe rank, book shelf etc, cos I read a lot.

5) I will also like to know if I can make an advance payment that will stand as a kind of commitment that I am truely coming over so you can hold the room down for me.

Waiting to hear from you…I am always online.

- Hanna

Subject: Apartment Details
From: BifidaHendrixMD@gmail.com

Dear Hanna,

Yes, the room is still for rent and you sound quite adequate. I'm glad to hear you're in the health care industry. I am a doctor of the spine, so I'm sure we'll have much to talk about. The room is already fully furnished, but I suppose you could put your organ in research room #6. I had it soundproofed a year ago on account of a new treatment I've been working on (although I must insist you play nothing in the key of C as I have patients with thinning ear drums).

Here are the apartment details:

1. The room is of average size (includes pillow, blanket, dresser, individual hand soap and alarm clock).

2. The monthly rent is $1,100 plus one month advance payable by personal check, money order, or cash. (This can be sent to me in advance to secure the room.)

3. Your car can be parked in the patient parking lot next to the clinic van.

4. The room is currently without a bookshelf, although I'm sure we could rig something up. Bruce, my orderly, is very handy.

P.S. The room does not come with a shoe rack, although we could use one considering there are extra bedroom slippers lying around from previous patients who didn't quite make it.

Sincerely,

Bifida Hendrix M.D.
Gentle Movements Spine Care Center

Subject: Payment Instructions
From: hanna_jones002@yahoo.com

Hello Dr. Bifida!

Thanks so much for the kind of mail that you just sent me. I want you to know what brought my attention to your advert is that you are a kind person and your replying to me is a thankful thing. I will do my possible best to make all processes you ask be answered and I will not hesistate to do what ever you tell me.

Concerning the payment, it will get to you as soon as I get your contact details and the full name which will be on the check, cus I like to do things in such a way as to be comfortable with whom I am working with. I also want you to know that in this transaction, I shall be trusting you. So I will like you to tell me some things about you which are neccesary for me to know. I hope to meet with you and have some time to get to know more about you, cus life depends on the interaction between people living in different locations.

Hoping that this medium gets to you in good condition of health. May the lord of hosts bless you more and more.

Regards from,

Hanna

Subject: Details
From: BifidaHendrixMD@gmail.com

Hanna,

You say you'd like to know more about me? Well, I'm a quiet person who enjoys polite conversation and growing ferns. I'm also head of the Chad Everett fan club. My practice, Gentle Movements Spine Care Center, is located in the rear of the house, so I really need a quiet tenant who will not disturb my patients. I am doing some very important research on bifurcated spinal columns and I have several of my research subjects living here at the clinic.

Please let me know when you will be arriving so I can move little Billy. He's making a fuss about being transferred to a smaller room, but considering his cerebral fits I think he would be better off away from the northern lights.

P.S. You can send the $2,200 check to me, Bifida B. Hendrix M.D. at the Spine Center (4432 S. Service Rd, Metarie, LA 70006).

Sincerely,

Dr. Bifida

Subject: Payment Instructions
From: hanna_jones002@yahoo.com

Hello Dr. Bifida,

I hope all is well. I had a dream of greatness in the future of life and it turned out to be you. But I will like you to do me a favour of which I will be much more than grateful. As soon as the check gets to you, I would like you to inform me cus I want to move to the States while the transaction is going on. I will be needing your help for that as I shall need money for my air bill and other things.

Will you please send me the sum of **$2,600 USD.** As soon as the payment is being cleared, you can deduct both the actual fee for the rent and then the fund I collected from you to pay for my air bill. I will be staying in a hotel till the check clears. This is because I am the kind of person who likes doing things in such a way that will favour other people, because I appreciate decency in all.

One more thing, I will like to know more about your private life cus there is a saying that says "all work and no play makes jack a doll boy." I want you to know that I am much excited to meet you, cus you sound like a real nice person indeed.

I pray the lord of hosts to bless you more and more in the eternity of life. At this point in time I would love to give you a call, but I can not due to certain reasons which is known only to me.

- Hanna

Subject: Money Situation
From: BifidaHendrixMD@gmail.com

Hanna, thanks for asking about my life. I don't get to share it much considering most of my patients are highly medicated. I really don't see a problem with the money situation, just send the check to me and we can work the rest out later.

You're absolutely right about that saying, I once had a psychiatric patient who was a "doll boy." It took me three years and a lot of Loxapine to convince him he wasn't married to Malibu Barbie. He's completely well now, but he still has a fixation for girls with tiny feet that smell like polyethylene.

I'm glad you're enthused about moving in with us, but I should warn you, things can get a little unpredictable here at the clinic. Last night I had my monthly fan club meeting and our topic for discussion was: "Which Was Better, Medical Center or Surfside 6?" It got very heated and I had to call in Bruce, my orderly, to calm things down. You wouldn't believe what that man can do with a hankie and some ether. You'll like Bruce, he has very strong hands.

I've decided to go ahead and use research room # 6 for your organ. Like I said, it's sound-proof so you can play as much as you want without disturbing any of the patients. I've been using it for a test subject who has duospinosis, a very rare disorder that involves the growth of a second spine. He's in phase 2 of his treatment and I think the lack of sunlight may be encouraging the growth of a third, at least that's what that extra shoulder nub tells me.

- Your Dr. Bifida

Subject: Payment Arriving Soon!
From: hanna_jones002@yahoo.com

Hello,

How you doing today? I hope you had a grate Sunday ahead of you. I will like to bring to your notice that your chek package will be getting to you sooner. That will be before Friday in probably two to three working days time. Also, I will like to hear from you as time goes on. Please do take note that I am counting on you for this payment process. - Hanna

---

Subject: I'll Be On The Lookout
From: BifidaHendrixMD@gmail.com

Hanna,

I must say, Sunday was above average, although it did have its low points. My patient Velma (research room # 4) suffered a slipped disc and I'm afraid it slipped so much Bruce had to retrieve it from behind the radiator. She's doing much better now thanks to my new invention, "The Vertebrizer" (see photo). I'm still waiting for the patent to clear, but when it does you can be sure it will be sold worldwide. It's the reinforced chin strap that makes it such a success.

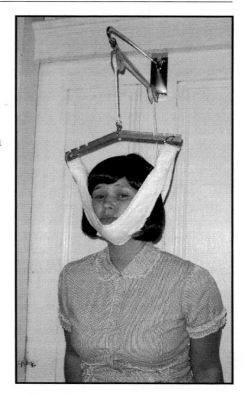

P.S. The patients and I eagerly anticipate your arrival. They don't see too many new folks and Velma wants to know if you like pie. She's trying to learn how to bake but her missing fifth vertebrae is making it difficult for her to roll dough. So, how do you feel about stewed prunes instead?

- Dr. B.

Subject: U Are Blessed
From: hanna_jones002@yahoo.com

Dr. Bifida,

In such a way you have talked, I must let you know that in my mind and spirit I am thinking of what you look like and that I can't wait to meet you in person.

All my life I have wanted to stay with a kind person who will be peacefull at all times and that is just the kind of person you are. I pray that the lord brings you the best of days as you step into the days of your life.

Well, please I will like to ask a favour from u ...Please as soon as you get the check, cus you are getting the check most likely today, please send me the sum of **$2,600 USD** so that I can move in by latest this Friday. Also, I would love to know if you and your family would have dinner with me. PLEASE LET ME KNOW IF THIS IS OKAY.

Regards from Hanna

Subject: See You This Weekend!
From: BifidaHendrixMD@gmail.com

Dear Hanna,

We would be delighted to have you for dinner this weekend. To celebrate your arrival, Velma is planning a very special meal so we've hooked up the Vertibrizer for her so she can stand at the stove. It's rigged to the ceiling fan by way of a pulley system. We tested it out for Thanksgiving and everything would have gone smoothly if Bruce hadn't flipped on the fan switch.

Because you were wondering what I look like, I'm including my picture. It was taken at my last spine conference where I was the keynote speaker. The topic was "Duospinosis at The Dow Plant: Was It Dursban That Made Billy Grow a Second Spine?" It was surprisingly well attended.

P.S. I haven't received the check yet, but I'm sure it will arrive shortly.

Your friend,

Dr. Bifida

Subject: Check Has Gotten To U Please Get Back To Me
From: hanna_jones002@yahoo.com

Dearest Bifida,

Thanks so much for the kind mail you have sent to me. I want to bring to your notice that the check payment has gotten to you and also I will like you to please get back to me as soon as possible cus I need to get to the States by Sunday the latest.

And please, also make sure that you get back to me as soon as you get this message cus I am really worried with the way you have not gotten back to me.

- Hanna

Subject: Check
From: BifidaHendrixMD@gmail.com

Dear Hanna,

I just want you to know that I am, indeed, getting back to you. I have not received the check yet, although Clermin (research room # 8) sometimes misplaces the mail. He doesn't mean to. In fact, ever since I installed the dual-valve spine tapper in his back hump his memory has improved dramatically. But come to think of it, he may be in need of another flushing.

It would be perfect for you to arrive on Sunday, that way you can have a nice dinner with us then sit in on our nightly therapy session. Velma has written a special song for you called "Moonbeams and Moist Kittens." (At least that's what I think she said. Sometimes her pinched discs affect her speech pattern.) Anyway, she hopes you will be able to accompany her on your organ. Later, we can all gather in the living room for episode # 33 of "Medical Center." It's the one where Doctor Gannon makes eyes at Nurse Chambers and Nurse Bascomb gets jealous.

P.S. Please send me a picture of yourself in your next email. Bruce has been asking me what you look like.

Your friend,

Dr. Bifida

Subject: My Picture
From: hanna_jones002@yahoo.com

Hello, how are you doing? With this mail is an attachment of my picture. I hope you like it cus that's the most current one I have. I want you to get back to me when u get the check cashed ok?

- Hanna

Subject: Bruce
From: BifidaHendrixMD@gmail.com

Dear Hanna,

Thanks for the photo, even though it's small, I'm afraid it has caused quite a stir at the clinic. It seems that Bruce is now quite taken with you. He's a nice boy, but he can be a bit impulsive. He's already making you a homemade greeting card with little hearts and arrows. I don't know where he learned the anatomy of the human heart, but the atriums and ventricles are amazingly accurate and who knows how he got the pericardium sac right.

That boy certainly can be crafty. He put on an entire puppet show last week and played all of the characters himself. It took him awhile to get the socks off his hands for the scene changes, but somehow it didn't affect the plot. He wants to know if you have a boyfriend in Africa, and if not, would you be interested in an American one.

P.S. Still no check. I wonder what the hold up could be?

- Dr. B

Subject: Well What Do I Have To Say Except Thank U
From: hanna_jones002@yahoo.com

Dr. Bifida,

I want you to know that in a case like this NOTHING OR ANYTHING IS EXPECTED FROM A PORR GIRL LIKE ME. I have been heart broken many times and that is the reason why I get afraid to get involved with any man. Even some of my friends say,"will I ever get married?" But I will let them know that when the right person meets me.

Well, how old is your son and what kind of job does he do?? All this I would like to know cus I have been in the fantacy dream of love life and that's just the fact of the matter. Also, I want you to know that in every relationship that I might be having with your son, it is based on the principle of knowledge and the fact that all should be well in due time. All I am saying is that we need to sit down and redifine our selves.

I wish that the check could just get to you right now so I could see what your son looks like and I could talk to him in person. I wish I could get to the phone now but these days things are not easy at all. So please, it would be best to do it this way. The very day that the check gets to you please do me a favour by sending me the difference so that I can make it to the States in about two days. That should be prisisely about $2,700 USD or less I guess.

Love and care to your son and regards to you from,

Hanna

Subject: Correction…
From: BifidaHendrixMD@gmail.com

Dear Hanna,

I'm sorry for the confusion. Bruce is my orderly, not my son. He simply helps out at the clinic with odd jobs and unruly patients. He is a delightful man though and I'm sure you two will hit it off quite well when you finally meet. He has never really dated girls before, but he's excited to see you. In fact, he's so excited he's decorating your room with construction paper angels. They're a bit hunched over, but since he was using Velma as a model I guess that stands to reason.

On another note, we are all very excited here at the clinic because it looks like my new therapeutic cream "Spine On" is going to have its patent approved. That means a big royalty check for me and presents for all of my patients who helped test it. Bernice is still recovering from a rather severe nerve rash from batch number 6 so I promised her something extra special. But I guess it's Clermin who gets the new clock radio since he came up with the product slogan, *"Don't moan, rub it on your back bone!"*

On a sad note, Billy, my duospinosis case, has taken a turn for the worse. It seems his second spine is angling in a northeastern direction, so I've had to direct his solar plexus towards Orion. But, if it's in the stars, he should make a full recovery by the next waning.

P.S. Bruce wants to know how you feel about Zapp's chips. He's making a portrait of you out of potato chips and Elmer's glue and he can't decide what kind of flavor to use for your hair. May I recommend Cajun Dill?

Yours,

Dr. Bifida

Subject: What Do I Have To Say Except God Bless U!
From: hanna_jones002@yahoo.com

Hello,

How are you doing today? I thank you so much for the kind of mail that you sent to me. In fact, I will like you to know that in such cases like this, things get more than decent with the opposite sex and that is why I will like to meet Bruce in person.

My check package ought to have arrived but due to the fact that my agent sent the fund into my account directly not knowing that I wanted it to be in the form of a check for someone special…that is the reason why it has not yet gotten to you. So I was hoping to let you know that by Friday latest you shall be getting the check package, and that is for sure cus I am doing all I can.

As soon as you get the check, please go and send me the difference so that I can complete my arrangment for coming over. Then myself and Bruce can go to the bank and get the check cleared. But if you don't mind, maybe you and I can just go to the bank and get it cleared.

I will like to have your cell fone number and I also wish to ask you out on a dinner evening when I get over and I just hope you can accept that from me.

Hoping that you have a great sunny feeling this morning. I am using this medium to tell you to have a nice day.

Regards from,

Hanna

Subject: Slight Trouble…
From: BifidaHendrixMD@gmail.com

Hanna, I wish I could say I'm having a "sunny feeling" this morning but I'm afraid I've encountered some difficulties in the development of my new back salve "Spine On." It seems to have caused some scarring in test subjects and I've been asked to re-mix the compound. Just when we thought we had a viable product, it looks like we need to start from scratch. My patients at the clinic are tired of being rubbed down with Noroxon-9 three times a day, and who can blame them? Bernice has developed lip boils and Velma's back skin is starting to come up in small sheets. Now it's my duty as a doctor to seek out new test subjects who aren't as sensitive to penetrative numbing agents. As a health care worker I'm sure you can relate to this dilemma.

I would give you my cell number but I'm afraid Velma "misplaced" my phone on account of her restless spine syndrome. Lately she's has a hard time keeping still, and I won't go into the details, but the phone flew out of the van window and is now somewhere out on I-10.

We were all very disappointed you were unable to make it here last weekend. We had a really big meal planned. Velma made her famous stuffed squash with turtle meat and Bruce put on a first-rate puppet show entitled, "Two Dress Socks Go To The Mall."

I do hope you'll be here by next weekend because Bruce does not deal well with disappointment. Ever since I lowered his Thorazine dosage he's had a problem with rage. Don't worry though, he weighs much less than he used to and he hasn't broken any furniture in at least three months.

Which reminds me, how do you feel about dating a man on psychotropic drugs?

P.S. I promised Bruce I'd send this picture to you. It's a puppet he made for you named "Squeezles the Love Sock."

Yours,
Bifida

Subject: Please See The Payment Is Coming
From: hanna_jones002@yahoo.com

Bifida,

Thanks so much for the kind mail you have sent to me. Please know that the payment will surely get to you by Monday so please take note of it.

I will also like to have dinner with you and Bruce, and that will be me cooking specifically for you, if you dont both mind. That would be mostly about Wednesday so when the check gets to you by Monday, please do make sure you send the fund the same Monday okay. I pray that the lord lets us meet in good health condition. Hoping to hear from you soonest.....

- Hanna

Subject: Favor?
From: BifidaHendrixMD@gmail.com

Hanna, I need to ask you a little favor. Because I have been running low on test patients lately for the back salve, I was wondering if you would be willing to volunteer your services in this department. I can assure you it is perfectly safe and I will even pay you $50 per treatment. I just need you to fill out this disclaimer form. It's simply for my records here at the clinic. If you agree, I will be happy to send you a cash advance for your trouble. You would really be doing all of us a great service, especially Billy, whose spine continues to angle dangerously to the northeast.

P.S. Bruce says hello. He's such a hard worker I've decided to give him a raise, as long as he keeps his eyes on the back dumpster. As a health care worker, I'm sure you know some things just weren't meant to live.

— Dr. B.

Medical Disclaimer Form # 338450
Gentle Movements Spine Care Center
Dr. Bifida Hendrix M.D. Certified Spineologist

Name _____Hanna Jones_____
Age _____28_____
Sex _____Female_____
Country of Origin __Lagos, Nigeria,_____
Occupation _____Health Care Worker_____
Current Activities____Hockey, Organ Playing_____

Have you ever experienced any of the following:
(Please check any that apply)

__ **Ringing in the Ears**   __ **Burning Urine**

__ **Shortness of Breath**   __ **Unusual Hair Growth**

__ **Skin Loss**   __ **Forked Tongue**

__ **Crossed Eyes**   __ **Undue Tanning**

__ **Spinal Leakage**   __ **Patchiness**

__ **Stumbling**   __ **Hip Dysplasia**

__ **Misplacement of**   __ **Exhaustion**
   a Major Organ

__ **Sensitivity to Noroxon-9**   __ **Dismay**

Signature _____

Subject: I Will Gladly Look Into It If U Accept This From Me
From: hanna_jones002@yahoo.com

Weeelllll!!! I just want you to know there is no need for you to ask me for that favour, it is already done. I dont mind signing the release for the clinic as soon as I get over there, but I would love it if I could get there as soon as possible to get this thing done. If you could just send me the fund now, when I get to the States I can give it back.

I hope that the lord always blesses you more and more in his infinite mercy.

Love and care from Hanna

Subject: Another Favor
From: BifidaHendrixMD@gmail.com

Hanna,

Thanks for agreeing to be a test subject. You can sign the release form when you arrive - that is if I'm still in business. You see, I'm afraid I've run into some trouble here at the clinic. The AMA is claiming the neurotoxins in my backbone salve instigated Velma's restless spine syndrome. This is crazy considering she was already quite restless in the first place (she couldn't walk through a room without taking down a set of drapes).

Anyway, I've been called to a hearing in Baton Rouge where I'm expected to present my case. If I win the hearing, I'll be able to continue working at the clinic, but if I lose, I could be convicted of malpractice and I'll lose my license.

I'm asking all of my patients to write a letter pleading my case. In fact, I wonder if you could write a short letter stating how I'm "a responsible professional who cares only about the advancement of medicine" and I in no way intend to "irreparably wound, damage, or inflict deadly chemicals on the spinal columns of my patients." As a health care worker, I'm sure a letter from you would help my case.

Bruce was so upset about all of this I had to sprinkle potassium bromide on his corn flakes. It calmed him down a little, but only after he kicked a hole through the side of the Spinerator. Now I don't know how Billy is going to get oxygen to vertebrae # 26.

I'll send you the money, but please Hanna, first help us out with a nice letter. Just don't mention anything about the dumpster out back. We don't need that headline in the paper again.

Yours in need,

Dr. Bifida

Subject: Dear Doctor Bifida
From: hanna_jones002@yahoo.com

Dearest Bifida,

Well, I want u to know this is a case we must win and now is the opportuniy we can help each other.

I have written a little note I feel should help but it would be nice if I get over to the States so we can get things done fast. I will like u to send me the funds so I can make arrangments for my flight. Can you get it sent today?

Please do take care of Bruce for me and make sure you put some calamine lotion on his body. I am sure that will calm him down. Here is the note….

Your loyal,

Hanna

Dear Sirs Regarding To Dr. Bifida:

It is with greatness in my mind that I write this short note to you. I would like you to understand that I am full of thanks to the Lord that Dr. Bifida has been a kind and honest person who would never do anything to harm others in any way. I must let you know that she has been able to save many patients who would have been dead by now in all ways if she did not try to save them.

It is a very sad thing if someone tries to charge her of an assult, cus due to what I know and what we all know, she is a good woman with a greatness in her mind. In the area of irreparable wounds or damages, she was trying to save things and was not intending to do things in such a bad way.

I will also like you to know that she made me realise there is more to life than everything in the world. While some people might think she was trying to get things wrong, I must let you know her role in society has helped much, so you should let her keep it up.

I have known her for not quite a long time but I appreaceat the way she has been running things in her place. This has also helped me as a doctor myself, and that is one of the greatest achievments in life.

Regards from,

Hanna Jones

Subject: Thank You For The Letter
From: BifidaHendrixMD@gmail.com

Dear Hanna,

Thank you so much, along with all of my patient's testimonials, yours was one of the kindest. I'm sure it will be quite effective in fighting my case. Instead of a letter, Bruce has decided to make a cardboard diorama of the clinic. He's quite a gifted artist, but I'm not sure what he plans to do with the decoupage hand turkey.

We're packing up the van for our trip, but I'm afraid we're already quite weighted down. The Spinerator's all steel construction could easily push the load to its maximum so we may need to pull it from behind with a rope.

P.S. Please give me your address so I can send the funds for your travel.

Wish us luck,

Dr. Bifida

Subject: Waiting For Western Union To Pick Up The Money
From: hanna_jones002@yahoo.com

Goood Morning Dr. Bifida,

I really appreceat the way you have mailed me. I want you to know I stand by you at all times and will make sure you get what you want. I want you to know that all will be well once you get back from this trip.

I solemly promise that in due time we shall make sure we get together to do things in such a way that will provide things in due time.

Please do take note that I am getting ready to come over to the States and move in and that is why I am asking you for the kind favour to send me **$1550 U.S.D.**

As soon as I get over both Bruce, you and I will spend much time together cus I think we really have things in common and I just want you to know that all in life is faith and knowledge of life. Please send the money via Western Union with this information to my flight agent:

Name = Trish Milton / Address = #24 Allen Road / City= Ikeja / State = Lagos / Country = Nigeria / Text question= Purpose? Answer = Clinic

Hoping to hear from you as soon as possible that all is okay.

Hanna

Subject: Very Urgent!
From: BifidaHendrixMD@gmail.com

Dear Hanna,

I need you to come to America at once! I've been detained in Baton Rouge for further questioning and there is no one to care for the patients at the clinic. Please, I beg you, I need a qualified health care worker to tend to them immediately - someone I can trust. If left alone Billy's condition may worsen and that will be the third tragedy research room # 9 has seen in 6 months!

The state has put a temporary freeze on my assets so you MUST find a way to get here by Tuesday. Little Billy's interior articular facets could fuse resulting in God knows what!

- Dr. Bifida

Subject: Urgent!! Please Send Money So I Can Get Moving Soon As Possible!!
From: hanna_jones002@yahoo.com

Hello My Dearest Friend,

I am so sorry, from the mail I read things are not going good. I think there must have been a misconception from the trial. I will still be needing $1550. USD to get my flight ticket so please go to the Western Union and get the fund sent so I can arrive by Thursday cus it would be a good thing for me to help out at the clinic with the patients.

I am also worried about you now myself and I need to get you out of this detention as soon as possible. Please dont let me wait long before I hear from you so I know all is okay.

Love and care from Hanna

Subject: My Situation…
From: BifidaHendrixMD@gmail.com

Dear Hanna,

Things here are very bad. My hearing turned into a three-ring circus and I am now being detained for further questioning. Truthfully, we had nothing but trouble from the start. Ever since the generator for Billy's Spinerator got lost on the highway we've been in bad shape. I told Bruce to use the sturdy rope but he was so busy gluing Cheerios to his diorama he apparently didn't listen.

I want you to know I presented your letter to the judge, although I'm afraid it was of little use after Velma's "incident." She tried her best to help my case by standing before the judges to testify, but her restless spine syndrome was so fierce she accidentally knocked over three folding chairs and a row of microphones.

Hanna, for the sake of little Billy, I gave the court your profile and they have agreed to allow a small fee for your services to come to America ($2,500) to attend the clinic. They just need to run a background check first to make sure everything is legal. Please give Officer Joe Cromwell a call and let him know you are a fully legitimate healthcare worker. He has been assigned to my case and can be reached anytime at (504) 399-****. And make sure to mention you are "one of the perfect workers at the hospital" just like you said in your first email to me.

With your help, I will get through this and practice medicine again. If not, God help us all.

Your friend,

Dr. Bifida

Subject: Please Act Fast On The Problem With The Phone Number!!
From: hanna_jones002@yahoo.com

Dr. Bifida,

I should let u know that Joe did not pick up the phone, even for a second time.

I ALSO WANT YOU TO KNOW IF YOU REALLY NEED MY HELP MAKE SURE YOU FIND A WAY TO SEND THE FUNDS CUS I WANT TO HELP YOU WITH ALL MY HEART AND MY PROFESSION!!!!

I dont mind rendring my help but it all depends on you okay? I am worried about you and Bruce. It makes me feel so sad that this thing is happeneing. I will try my best to help you out but make sure you send the money today cus I have already packed my things. I am making some documents that should be able to get you out of that place and help you to gain your proffesion back and make you safe for life.

If you can, get Bruce to send the funds from his own pocket then when I get over and work for the clinic I can pay him back, okay. **BUT MAKE SURE YOU SEND THE MONEY TODAY!!!!!!**

Love,

Hanna

Subject: Dear God Send The Documents ASAP!
From: BifidaHendrixMD@gmail.com

Hanna,

The state has informed me they will need to see your documentation papers before they will allow me to send you money for travel. Please email me something that states you are a certified health care worker. Anything will do – a certificate, a pay stub, even a crude drawing of the central nervous system.

Please Hanna, we are all relying on you. If nothing else, do it for little Billy. His articular facets are rapidly joining and if you don't get to him soon his back bone will surely ossify!

P.S. Officer Cromwell's phone is no longer in service. Due to an unfortunate misfiring incident at a public school he was taken off the force and I have yet to receive a replacement.

In haste,

Dr. Bifida

Subject: SITUATION OF THINGS - I NEED YOUR RESPONSE ASAP!!!!!
From: hanna_jones002@yahoo.com

Doctor,

I want you to know that all my credentials can not be placed cus I had to send them to the States about a month ago becose I needed to treat some people from Wiscousin. That was what I wanted to explain to the man you told me to call until I tried the number and it did not go through.

You also mentioned Billy and I am getting more and more sad about this cus I feel so much simpathy for him in all ways. The funniest thing is I know what it will take for him to get well and that is sure for me.

You will have to see that you get the funds sent today at all cost. Let them know that you have every thing under control and we have talked about this. I am hoping you understand what I am saying. Please make sure you get this done cus Billys life is in your hand and only I can help him right now.

I am online right now waiting for you to get back to me!

Subject: WHAT!!!!!!!
From: BifidaHendrixMD@gmail.com

Hanna, how can I send the funds when my assets have been frozen by the state of Louisiana? You said you were "making some documents to help me gain my profession back" and now you say they're in Wisconsin? I've already told you the court needs to see them before they will allow me to send the money!

YOU ARE WASTING VALUABLE TIME! BILLY WILL DIE IF YOU DO NOT HELP US IN OUR HOUR OF NEED!

Now hop to it and get on a plane right now or I will be forced to report you to the Medical Board of Nigeria. Believe me, if little Billy develops a cleft coccyx and his spinal fluid leaks all over the linoleum, I'm personally holding you responsible!!!!!

Sometimes I question whether you're in the medical industry at all.

- The Doctor

Subject: WHATS GOING ON????????????
From: hanna_jones002@yahoo.com

I want you to know I should not be in this position, I am not sure I can take this anymore. I am ready to help and if you feel you need my help for real, I will get over there when you send the funds!

I am getting tired of all these mails about me showing some proof. I mean how would I have lied in all the mails I have sent you?

If you report me to the medical association in Nigeria they will do me no harm at all and I will practice my proffesion to the fullest. That is cus I gave you the best option and you did not even try to get anything done. I must let you know I have been practicing my proffesion since I was just 21 years old and have gotten many awards from it and no one has ever died in my hands.

As you talk about Billy, I am getting more sad. If you really know how much he matters to you then you will find a way to send the money! Think well, cus if care is not taken we will be loosing him.

-Hanna

Subject: Now Look Here Woman...
From: BifidaHendrixMD@gmail.com

Hanna,

I'm afraid your constant dawdling has put us in a critical position. Because you disobeyed my orders to come to his need, Billy's coccyx has not only become cleft, it has morphed into two vestigial tailbones that move independently and with great fury. He was rushed to Tulane Hospital late last night and I'm afraid the news is grim. The truth is, he was left unattended for too long and his prognosis is unclear. This photo shows only the hopelessness on his face and not the ungainly tailbones that are quickly taking over his small frame.

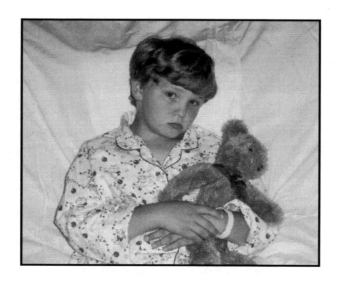

Hanna, because I hold you personally responsible for this tragedy, I'm going to be sending you his medical bills (including the stuffed bear and custom-made jammies with tail holes.)

How could you have done this? We considered you a close friend, almost part of the family. I was even offered a $2,000 increase on your travel expenses by the state! Bruce is heartbroken and so is the Chad Everett Fan Club. They were relying on you to host the next meeting which was going to feature episode 18 of Medical Center - "A Duel With Doom." Now what are they going to do? Bernice made Chex mix and everything!

I hope you don't treat your patients in Africa they way you treat us. If so, heaven help us all.

- Dr. Bifida

Subject: Please Forgive Me For What I Said The Other Time
From: hanna_jones002@yahoo.com

Well I must let you know the picture I am seeing here makes me feel so sad I have not even tried to eat nor sleep since morning due to the fact that I am guilty of this. I tried to pray to God for firgivness and I sure hope he forgives me.

I got some money from a friend which would only help with half the amount I would need which is $500 USD. So I will like you to know that all I need now is about $1,150 USD.

For me, little Billy is like my son. I look at him like I have hurt my own heart. I just want you to know you should be the one to help me out now cus I feel I am the one that truely gave birth to him and I must not let him die.

I don't want Bruce to think that I am a bad fellow, so please send the funds so I can arrive by Tuesday and get little Billy treated. I hope you understand what I mean cus I feel like I am responsible for everything to save little Billys dear life.

I LOVE BRUCE, BUT MOST OF ALL I LOVE BILLY!!!!

Love and prayers from,

Hanna

Subject: Very Bad News
From: BifidaHendrixMD@gmail.com

Hanna,

This is very difficult for me to say, but little Billy is dead. It seems his tiny body was unable to handle the stress of being duospinated and he gave up the will to live at 4 a.m. this morning. We are all in a great deal of shock from this tragedy and it has not been easy to cope. Bruce is beside himself, Velma has been institutionalized, and considering Clermin was forced out of our backup Spinerator by the state medical examiners, we were afraid we would lose him as well. They claimed it was a "dangerous contraption made of metal tubing, rusted bolts and various household appliances." But just because a machine is powered by a crock pot element doesn't mean it can't save someone's life.

Hanna, I hope you realize all of this happened because of you. If you had just gotten on that plane instead of constantly asking for travel money little Billy would still be alive. How will you live with yourself now?

P.S. I had the good sense not to tell Bruce that you are a "fellow," as you stated in your last email. I'm afraid he is still very much in love with you and any news of a transgender situation would surely induce a breakdown. I want you to know I have treated many multiple-sexed individuals and I can assure you it is nothing to be ashamed of. With a little Trazodone and a nice dress, you can feel like the girl you've always longed to be.

Say a prayer for little Billy. He's in heaven now with all of God's other two-tailed children.

- Dr. Bifida

Subject: Bruce's Request
From: BifidaHendrixMD@gmail.com

Hanna,

Despite everything, Bruce is insisting I send you money to attend Billy's funeral. Would you be able to make it here by Saturday?

- The Doctor

Subject: Yes, I Will Come!
From: hanna_jones002@yahoo.com

Dr. Bifida,

Well ....I am really short of words and do not know what to say. Please try to understand that I am not happy with what happened and I prayed for Billy and in all ways I am sorry for his death, but the lord has ways of doing things.

I would love to come over Saturday if it comes from your mind to get the money sent. As soon as you get it sent, I will be heer waiting to recieve the Western Union information. I sure hope that you get back to me with the information today.

I HOPE YOU TELL BRUCE I AM ON THE WAY. MAKE SURE YOU SEND ME THE EXACT AMOUNT....OKAY?

-Hanna

Subject: Billy's Funeral Expenses
From: BifidaHendrixMD@gmail.com

Hanna,

We've arranged Billy's funeral and I'm afraid it's going to cost quite a bit more than we anticipated. Bernice is planning the service at Myron Murmelstein's

House of Eternal Rest and she's insisting on many extras that she feels little Billy deserves. (I told her paying $2,000 for a Mickey Mouse impersonator was a bit high, but she just won't budge.)

Because my assets are still frozen by the court, I think it's only fair that you pay for the down payment on the funeral bill. After all, if you had been able to make it to the clinic in time this whole disaster would never have happened.

I'm including the bill below. Please try to get the money here by Friday so we can pay for the special-order coffin. We're having one built with an extra side extension for Billy's tailbones.

I'm afraid Bruce had a seizure when I told him you weren't a "straight" woman, but I don't want you to worry, you two probably weren't right for each other anyway. There will be several other trans-gendereds at the service so you needn't feel uncomfortable.

P.S. Please try to bring some mouse ears. We're having a theme funeral and I want to make sure you fit in with the other guests.

Yours in grief,

Dr. Bifida

HOUSE OF ETERNAL REST FUNERAL PARLOR

Attending Director: Mr. Myron Murmelstein
"Putting your mind at rest in times of stress"

Bill of Services for: Billy Wainwright

General Embalming: $800.   Formalin Compound-W
Black Funerary Suit: $150.   Size 3 Petite w. Shoe
Novelty Mouse Ears: $138.   8 dozen
Mouse Impersonator: $2,000 Tip Not Included
Casket Preparation: $115   Twice-Rubbed Oak
Casket Extension: $358. Special Order
Flower Arrangements: $331. Magnolias w. Spray
Novelty Pallbearer Suits: $949. "Goofy" "Daffy"
                              "Dumbo" and "Tweety"
Disney Royalty Fee: $599.
Internment Fee: $49.
Memorial Stone: $499. "Mighty Morphin' Power
                            Ranger"
Memorial Shrub: $22.   Evergreen Topiary
                            Dancing Bear
Gravedigging Fee: $98.   Mini Bulldozer Reserved
Misc. $157. Balloon Sculpting with
                            Buzzy The Clown

Total Charge: $6,265   10% deposit required =$626.50

Subject: I Have Had Enough Of This!
From: hanna_jones002@yahoo.com

At this point in time I am very disapointed in you. You should think of your self as an incompitent woman cus you dont know your duty as a doctor! I see now you dont even want to send the money!

GET THIS INTO YOUR BRIAN, I DID NOT CURSE ANY PROBLEMS FOR YOU OK!

That is all!

Subject: WHAT!!!!!
From: BifidaHendrixMD@gmail.com

HANNA, YOU ARE A CRUEL AND HEARTLESS "WOMAN" AND I HOPE FOR YOU'RE SAKE YOU NEVER DEVELOP TWO VESTIGIAL TAIL BONES!!!!!

How dare you call me an incompetent doctor! I've always strived to advance medicine in the most humane way possible, just ask my patients. If I hadn't picked Billy up from that drainage ditch behind Drago's Oysters he surely would have perished years ago. At least with my care he was able to enjoy his short life to the fullest.

Please Hanna, just stay in Africa. When the state releases me on bond I'm going to remodel your bedroom and use it for Officer Cromwell. He's got a pain in his lower lumbar that I'm quite sure is mad back disease. Of course, I won't be sure until the new moon begins to wane.

P.S. I'm including a photo of little Billy's mother at the funeral. It was a beautiful service with clowns, balloons and all of the Disneyland characters. The costs were exorbitant, but I'm sure we'll find a way to pay for it somehow.

- Dr. Bifida Hendrix M.D.

Chapter 7.

Danny Wingnuts

Subject: Danny Wingnuts
    (Paint Shop Clerk, Football Fanatic)

Con Man: Ibrahim Isa
    (Nigerian Football Star Seeking Manager)

Attempted swindle: $3,500

Subject: Help A Footballer In Need
From: ibrahimisa_500@yahoo.com

Dear Sir,

Please permit me to introduce myself, my name is Ibrahim Isa. I originated from the Sokoto State of Nothern Nigeria. I am a young man of 21yrs and still single. I am a footballer by profession. I have played with one of the most popular and leading teams in Nigeria named ABIOLA BEST of Abeokuta. That was in the year 2004.

I am a full midfeilder and I have captained this team through out my stay. I left the ABIOLA BEST in the June 2005 due to an injury. I felt so humiliated during this period because I was abandoned due to Nigerian politics in football. I was the best midfeilder in my team until my injury time.

However, I happened to consult the Nigerian Football Association (NFA) whom later came to my rescue at the hospital. Now I have fully recovered from my injury and the ABIOLA BEST of Abeokuta needs me back again. But I will rather choose to quit football than to play for that team again. That is why I am soliciting for a new foreign team either a European, American, Australian or Asian team. Hence I will need someone to call my manager.

As soon as my Manager can fix me with a good team, whatever money that is being paid on my behalf I wouldn't mind sharing at the percentage of 60% for my Manager and 40% for myself. He is going to take the responsibility of my trip to his country or wherever he desires me to play.

If this proposal is acceptable by you, please don't hesitate to reply to me through this email address. I will be looking forward to hearing from you. May Allah bless you. - Ibrahim Isa

Subject: Heck Yeah, I'd Love To Help!
From: TheWingnutWay@gmail.com

Dude, that is so cool, I'm way into football too! I'd be happy to help you out and talk to you about your time in the league.

That injury sounds harsh, but I think I know what you're going through. I popped my anterior cruciate back in high school, that's why I never made it to the NFL. Believe me, if that bonehead towel boy hadn't left those wet rags on the floor I would be in the big time for sure. But don't get me wrong, that doesn't mean I'm not totally qualified to work with you. I've been assistant manager of Glidden Paint for 6 years now, so it's not like I don't know what I'm doing.

- Danny Wingnuts

Subject: THANK YOU!
From: ibrahimisa_500@yahoo.com

Sir,

Thanks for your response, I appreciate the fact you have accepted to help me in my football career. I promise to do my best in making sure that your effort towards me will never be in vain. I will like you to give me details of your profile, everything about yourself including your picture for my perusal so I can be very sure of whom you are.

It will now be your duty to direct me on how to get prepared for my trip to your country so we can meet face to face. I will be needing to submit my Intl. passport and other traveling documents to the embassy of your country to enable me to procure my visas. Therefore I will also be needing some financial assistance. As you know, I just recovered back to my fit and have spent virtually all my savings.

At the time being, I will like you to iniciate the sum of **$3,500** through Western Union Money Transfer. Please initiate the money in favour of my identity: **Ibrahim Isa / Kaduna Nigeria.**

Please feel free to call me on my direct telephone: +2348029413367 for some vibral discussions on how to actualize this exercise. I will be very greatful if my request is greatly considered by you. In case you need to know, I am a very straight forward person who likes to have something doing with very honest and transparent people, which I believe you must be one.

I shall be looking forward to hearing from you shortly.

- Ibrahim Isa

Subject: A Few Ideas...
From: TheWingnutWay@gmail.com

Hey Ibrahim,

It's good to hear from you man. I want you to know you made the right decision choosing me as your manager. You said you wanted "details of my profile." Well, all you really need to know is that I'm an avid Steelers fan and I pretty much know everything there is about football. Just to prove how hardcore I am, here's a picture of me at the last home game.

I've been thinking, if you want to be a success, we really need to get you on a team in America. On the other hand, maybe we should just rock out and create one of our own. I've got a few ideas about team names and stuff but I haven't nailed anything down yet. I could probably help you out with expenses, as long as you're solid on the 60% cut.

Before we do anything, I have to insist you get back into peak performance shape, so I drew up a little something I call the "Wingnut Muscleblitz Explosion." It focuses on three important factors of the Wingnut vision. 1. Hard work. 2. Diligence. 3. Muscles exploding in an array of ferociousness.

No matter what, make sure to do some of these key endurance exercises every day, ok?

- 50 rear end shuttle sprints
- 20 minutes of high knee running, jumping and hopping
- 32 laps of jogging backwards (full uniform required)
- 149 two-footed triaxal thrusts
- 50 north-facing biflexal curls
- And as many rear lunges as your body can take before you either pass out or hurl

This all takes lots and lots of D-I-C-I-P-L-I-N-E. But without it we'll be no better than a bunch of girls running around chasing butterflies and whippoorwills. And don't worry about the money, I've got that covered. I just need to work a few things out at the Glidden shop.

Always remember Ibby, you gotta FIGHT and you gotta fight HARD. Not so hard that you tear anything major, but hard enough so you win, ok bro?

Let me know if you come up with any names for the team. I'm sure there are plenty of opportunities here in Pennsylvania where we can get a group together and really rock out.

Living for the dream!

Danny Wingnuts - Manager

Subject: Greetings From Your Player
From: ibrahimisa_500@yahoo.com

Hi Danny,

After a careful study of your message I was able to figure out some reasonable thoughts from you. I will also like to thank you very much for the informational data about yourself.

I am very impressed with your promises on how you will be making arragements in raising the fund for my trip to your country. I am also very glad for all the advice and the list of exercises to be done. I am making you a promise that they must be done as you have instructed to enable me to return fully back to my fit.

I realize that fitness matters a lot in the game, otherwise I will look no better than a bunch of girls running around chasing butterflies and whippoorwills, just like you have said. I want to inform you that I will never slumber in any of my activities so we can actualize our dream.

Considering the area you have requested of me to come up with some name for the team, I don't think I am in the position to do that, I suggest you do that yourself.

I will be waiting until I hear from you. But please, whatsoever is to be done must be done faster to help in facilitating my arrangements.

Thank you,

Ibrahim Isa

Subject: A Crapload of Plans...
From: TheWingnutWay@gmail.com

Hey Ibby,

Great news! I've come up with a totally cool name for the team. My buddy Carlos liked the name "Power Stroke" but after a lot of thought I think "Firedogs" would be best. (And just so you know, the name came to me when my dog Frank took a righteous piss on a fire truck, it's not like I set him on fire or anything.)

We came up with some drawings last night during a strategy session. Carlos drew this one up on a cocktail napkin. I guess he was a little drunk at the time, that's why it looks more like a flaming potato than a real dog.

And another thing, the more I think about it, the more I realize we're going to need to get a private jet or something. We're gonna be playing so many games we won't have time to drive all the way from Shanksville to Tuscaloosa and stuff. Like I said, don't worry about the travel funds, Carlos and I are devising a game plan and I think we cooked up something pretty good.

Like Dick Vermeil says, "Look up, lock down, and launch hard." So launch hard bro. Just make sure you don't launch your knee socket out of whack because that shit costs money.

P.S. Send me some pictures of your torso so I know how cut you are. Remember, you gotta be able to take 350 pounds flying at you like a cement truck on a grease spill.

Danny - Firedogs Manager

Subject: I Am Very Much In Liking
From: ibrahimisa_500@yahoo.com

Dear Sir,

I am really impressed with your response and all the good efforts you have comitted towards the progress and reality of our team. Thanks for helping me get back my destiny again, may the Almighty God reward you.

Secondly, I think you made a very nice choice in the discovery of a name for our team - like you said, Fire Dog. The name comes up with so many meanings. Fire is very delegate and dogs are always very agile.

Here is the picture which you asked me to send.

Your obedient,

Ibrahim

Subject: Plans of Facilitation
From: TheWingnutWay@gmail.com

Ibby dude, thanks for the picture, but what's with all the soccer players? Do you think these guys could learn football and join our team? They don't look very cut, but I guess we could beef them up with some milk shakes or something.

Hey, I've got good news. Carlos and I have a strategy all mapped out on how to get our start up money. Dude, it's going to be righteous, we're going to use a totally triple-pronged approach. We're gonna call it "Operation Housepaint."

Here's how it will work. Tomorrow at midnight I'm going to wear dark clothes and sneak into the Glidden shop. While I'm breaking into the register and stuffing cash into a pillowcase, Carlos will be waiting in the getaway car with a six-pack and some post victory snacks. If anyone approaches and threatens our plan, he'll just flash his mondo jailhouse pecs. We're even gonna use his souped-up Ram Van. It's got a butt-load of secret tear-away paneling and check out the bullet-proof tires…

Wish me luck bro. By this time tomorrow we should be up to our eye holes in football dough.

Your manager,

Wingnuts!

Subject: I Am Praying
From: ibrahimisa_500@yahoo.com

Dear Manager Wingnuts,

I wish you the best of luck in your plan. Like I have promised you before, I will never let you down or disappoint you in anyway. I have prayed to God to provide you with money to facilitate our dream to reality.

Your obidient servant Ibrahim

Subject: Ok…here's the thing
From: TheWingnutWay@gmail.com

Now Ibby, I don't want you to panic, but it turns out Carlos is not exactly the kind of offensive player I thought he was. In fact, he's kind of a chowder head.

"Operation Housepaint" didn't exactly turn out as smoothly as we had hoped. How was I supposed to know the cash drawer would be empty at night? It's not like I'm *head* manager or anything. Anyway, we weren't going to let a little failure stand in our way, so last night we launched directly into Plan B.

Well, Plan B, which was supposed to "score big bucks and choice chicks" turned into a big crap sandwich pretty much from the get go. Carlos was totally confident holding up the drive through at Taco Bell would work (and it would have too if he hadn't huffed so much Krylon and left the hold-up gun on the toilet). So like a couple of jackasses there we were at the late-night drive through asking the taco kid for all of his cash - *without even having a weapon!* So not only did we *not* get any money out of the robbery, Carlos kept coughing up lung spooge and the dude at the window wouldn't sell us gorditos because it was after 3!

But listen, as your manager, I don't want you to be discouraged. I refuse to be called a quitter, that's just not the Wingnut way. If you'll let me work on another game plan I swear I can get stratified. If I don't, you can come to my house and personally kick the living shit out of me. In fact, as your manager, I would insist on it.

You gotta keep the faith bro, I promise I won't let you down this time. Keep it tight, but not too tight, ok?

- Wingnuts

Subject: Look
From: ibrahimisa_500@yahoo.com

Hey Dude,

I have had enough of this. I don't understand this drama any more. I am fading and tired of your stories. You have made me lose hope with you so I have started up myself with a new team. I have already told the new manager everything about myself and he has assured to be of help.

I wouldn't like to miss this very life time opportunity just because of you. Therefore if you are very sure that you can not make it up to me, please I would appreciate you to declare your true intentions. That will enable me to ease myself and find a team to keep myself going. Or do you just want to ruin my future carrier?

It is obvious that you have asked for a second chance, and your request is granted. Please don't forget this year is almost coming to it's expiration, therefore whatever you do should be done fast without further delay.

As you can see I am running out of patients as time waits for no one.

Ibrahim Isa

Subject: HOLY CRAP ON A CRACKER!
From: TheWingnutWay@gmail.com

Ibby,

Look, I know you're pissed, but as your manager I HAVE TO TELL YOU THE GREATEST NEWS YOU'RE EVER GONNA HEAR IN YOUR LIFE!!!!!!

Don't ask me how I did it, but I got you a try-out for offensive tackle with the Mississippi Mudcats. Can you believe it? After a lot of phone calls I finally got through to the assistant coach. I told him how famous you are in Africa and everything and he's really excited to see your moves. He's cleared his schedule and set up a time for us next week. This is going to launch your career so hard and fast you'll think you were hit with a flaming meteor covered in pure liquid fire.

If we're going to be a winning team, we've got to watch our budget and I decided $3,500 was way too much to spend on a plane ticket, so I found a cheaper one online. I'm including the flight information below, all you have to do is pack your uniform and pads and get yourself to the airport. I talked Carlos into selling his brother's Camaro so I had enough to buy it. And don't worry about money for food and stuff, as your manager, I'll cover all of that.

I'll pick you up at the airport in Pittsburgh, then we'll all drive down there in the Ram. It's got a mattress in back so you'll have plenty of room to stretch out your ligaments. Can't wait to see you man, this is going to be HUGE!

	United Flight 9021 operated by Lufthansa / Flight 945 / 734	11:15pm Lagos, Nigeria (LOS)	4:03pm - Sun, Dec 31 Next day arrival Pittsburgh , PA (PIT)	22hrs 48mi n - 2 Stops Change planes in Frankfurt, Germany (FRA) Change planes in Chicago, IL (ORD)	$2,396 per person

Subject: Manager, This Is Urgent
From: ibrahimisa_500@yahoo.com

Dear Manager,

I am very surprised at your message and I am a little confused about this arrangement. I have observed a careful study of the ticket and I think you should realize that I don't like the idea. Sunday is just 2 days away. Yet you need me to board while I have seen no arrangement for money yet. Is this the right way to follow up this contract?

Please, I need you to speak to my understanding. Why don't you provide me your telephone number so that we can talk over the phone?

- Ibrahim

Subject: Don't Worry So Much…
From: TheWingnutWay@gmail.com

Dude, what's there to talk about? It's the Mississippi Mud Cats man, they're hard core! This is the break we've been looking for. All you have to do is pack a duffle bag and get on that plane, me and Carlos will be waiting for you at the airport. We'll be the ones with the big banner that says "Wingnuts Sports Management." Plus, we just shaved our heads in honor of Ben Roethlisberger's burst appendix so you can't miss us.

I told you not to worry about money. We still have $1,000 left over from the sale of the car, so we'll have plenty of cash for traveling in style. I plan on steak dinners and top shelf beer the whole way. So get yourself ready for the "U.S.A Wingnut Football Extravaganza Experience of a Lifetime." I just know you're gonna rock the house. And don't forget to bring some warm pants, those little African grass shorts aren't gonna cut it here dude, I think it's supposed to snow.

Your manager – bigger than life itself,

Wingnuts!

Subject: What?
From: ibrahimisa_500@yahoo.com

Mr. Manager,

I have told you to stop wasting my time because time is money. If you know you are not serious with this business, why don't you tell me in black and white so that I can find something better to do with my life!!

I am asking for your telephone number but instead all you do is tell me some bullshit that I don't understand. Do you expect me to fly from Kaduna to the Murtala Mohammed International Air Port Lagos after I have explained to you how financially set-back I am?

Come on, you need to reason with me. I am still a young star with a bright future. If you are not up to something, please I will advice we call it a quit at this point.

I like straight forward people. If that is you then why don't you send the money so that I will be coming to your country by Tuesday?

- Ibrahim

Subject: Dude...
From: TheWingnutWay@gmail.com

Ibby,

What is this, "send money so I will be coming to your country by Tuesday" crap? Don't you know our tryout with Coach Wringley is on Tuesday? It's like you don't want to cooperate with me at all. Haven't I told you about a million times I'm stratified? I know sports stars can be fickle, but you're making me crazier than a fruit bat on a bag of lemons.

Look, to play football in America you need to be a team player and asking for money all the time isn't going to score any touch downs. I don't think Frenchy Fuqua asked Terry Bradshaw for pocket change during the "Immaculate Reception." And if he did, he probably doesn't have any teeth now because of it.

I don't want to fight, alright? For a $100 change fee I can get you on a flight later today, but that means we've got to high-tail it right from the airport to Tupelo. No stops for steaks, girls, truck stop showers or anything else fun we had planned, ok?

Dude, I'm warning you, this is the last time I'm going to change my plans for you. I've had this whole thing whacked out on paper for a long time and I really can't afford to deviate. Don't push me, you don't want to see Wingnuts gone wild.

I've got a 2:50 P.M. flight all lined up for you (United # 983). As your manager, I insist you arrive on time and well rested. I'll give you some spending money when you get here. Me and Carlos will be waiting at your gate in Pittsburgh with some liverwurst and a protein smoothie. Do NOT disappoint me.

P.S. I kinda told the coach you're the nephew of Nelson Mandela, so if he asks, just run with it, ok? Hey, you do speak English right?

- Manager Wingnuts

Subject: Ibby, You Failed Me
From: TheWingnutWay@gmail.com

Ibby,

Where in the hell were you?!!! We waited for you at the Pittsburgh airport for 6 goddamn hours! I can't believe you bailed on me after all I have done for you. I hate to say it dude, but that shit is indicative. I should have known you don't have what it takes. I was completely committed to raising money for our future career and getting us into the spotlight, but you went ahead and ruined it all! With that kind of behavior you'd never be a true Firedog.

As furious as I am at you, I still see a light at the end of the tunnel. Maybe if I can't trust you to come here, I should meet you in Nigeria where I can get some real action out of you. I could be there by next week. I've still got some money left over from the car sale, plus I could get the security deposit back from my apartment. After all, I wouldn't really need to live there anymore if I'm crunching deals over in Africa, right?

P.S. Remember what the great Vince Lombardi said, "Football is like life – it requires hard work, sacrifice and the ability to not screw over Wingnuts even when you know he's completely stratified."

- Your Manager

Subject: You are not a couch or manager for real
From: ibrahimisa_500@yahoo.com

Dudu,

You have to put a stop to all this. You must send money or I have to get a club of my chouse! If you are really a couch send me the money today!

- Ibrahim

Subject: What?
From: TheWingnutWay@gmail.com

Ibby, I don't understand what the hell you're talking about. "Couch" "Dudu"? Have you been smoking banana leaves?

Subject: I Am Here!
From: ibrahimisa_500@yahoo.com

No my manager, I am not smoking banana leaves. I am now in Mortala Muhamed Airport Lagos, so you have to send me the money, even $500 is ok for me. But make sure you wait for me at the airport, ok? Help me so that I will get to your country in time!

Subject: YOU'RE AT THE AIRPORT???
From: TheWingnutWay@gmail.com

Ok dude, I don't know how I would send money to an airport so just **GET ON THAT PLANE AND GET OVER HERE!** I'll go get Carlos, I think he's outside sleeping in a bush.

Subject: Plese Help
From: ibrahimisa_500@yahoo.com

ATTENTION:

Please my manager, I am in a very bad condition now as I am writing you. A good man just took me to his house because I didnt know what to do in the airport. The man gave me the $500.

You must give him the money back so that I can book another flight tomorrow. Come to the airport and wait for me. Look for his name…

1 Chukwunyere Okoronkwo
2 Lagos Nigeria
3 Use Western Union Money Transfer

Use this name and give him the money and call me to conferm. This is my number 2348029413367.

THANK YOU!

- Ibrahim

Subject: Dude, Who Is This Man?
From: TheWingnutWay@gmail.com

Ibby,

As your manager, I really don't think you should be hanging out with strange men you meet at the airport ok? Did you ever stop to think this dude could be out to kidnap you and hold you up for ransom so he can get mondo bucks to fly to Panama to buy drugs and silencers and stuff?

I think you may be in great danger Ibby. Look, I saw an episode of The Dukes of Hazard once where Luke kicked the living shit out of some dude's trachea. My advice is try that, ok?

Your manager,

Danny Wingnuts

Chapter 8.

Jr. Samples Jr.

Subject: Junior Samples Jr.
    (Used Car Dealer, Moonshine Fancier)

Con Man: Bill Arvin
    (Overseas Automobile Broker)

Attempted Swindle: Undetermined Amount, Possible Identity Theft

---

For Sale: 1992 Chevy Chagrin - $900
This vehicle is in tip-top shape, 190,000 miles,
Whitish in color, a real good driving machine.
Please contact **SamplesCarLot@gmail.com**
No hooliganry or funny business allowed. No foolin'.

Subject: '92 Chevy Chagrin - $900
From: b_arvin@rediffmail.com

Greetings friend,

My name is Bill Arvin, I have a company who is interested in buying your item. They informed me that the payment will be remmited via company check. Is the price listed firm? In order to conclude the deal as soon as possible, the check will be sent to you and will include the money for the sale of your item and the shippers fees for organising a home pick up service.

You do not need to worry as my shipping company will come to pick the item up from your base. You will be able to send the shipping charges to the shipping agent through Western Union money transfer as soon as you get the check. Then you can deduct the money for the sale of your item.

If you agree to assist in this capacity, kindly send your full name, address and your contact phone numbers. I will be waiting to read from you as soon as possible today so that we can proceed with this transaction.

- Bill Arvin

Subject: Chevy For Sale
From: SamplesCarLot@gmail.com

Bill,

Let me tell you right off I like your style. I am a man of fast business and straight deals, that's why Samples Car Lot has the best reputation in the used car industry.

I want you to know this particular vehicle is a special one on the lot. There were only 65 Chevy Chagrins made that year, then they were discontinued for having a faulty break line. But don't you worry, this one's been fixed up and stops on a dime, that's a Samples promise. I don't see any problem with paying the shipping fee as long as I receive a check for the vehicle promptly. You can send it to this address:

Samples Car Lot
Junior Samples Jr.- C.E.O (that just means "in charge")
701 Lemon Field Way Cumming, Georgia 30028
1-800-BR-549

I've put a real good spit shine on her which practically blinded everyone on the lot. (That's just a little joke, at Samples Car Lot no one ever gets hurt, at least not permanently.)

I'm also including a pint of our home-brewed "Samples Skull Whack." As you can see it's got a tar pitch base with a foam-free top.

We make it in back of the machine shop for lunch-time libations and de-greasing rear axles.

Let me know if you'd prefer a case.

Your man,

Junior Samples Jr.

(but my friends call
 me Jr. Jr.)

Subject: Please Mark Item
From: b_arvin@rediffmail.com

Mr. Jr. Jr.

I got your information and I have forwarded your name and address to the company for the check to be issued and sent to you.

I want you to be sure the item will be marked SOLD for my client. What I want to clarify is that will you be able to send the shipping charges to the shipping agent through Western Union Money Transfer method as soon as you get and cash the check. I will be waiting to read from you.

- Bill

Subject: Ok, Let's Lock Her Down!
From: SamplesCarLot@gmail.com

This all sounds like a done deal to me. I've already put her out on the street so you can drive off nice and easy.

By the way, I was going to give her a tune-up, but me and the boys got a little dizzy on the panther sweat (a.k.a. whoop juice of the homemade variety) and it sort of slipped our minds. But, I guess I could knock $20 dollars off the price. You see son, that's the kind of deals we make at Samples Car Lot – always fair, always square.

-Jr. Jr

Subject: What ??????
From: b_arvin@rediffmail.com

I don't understand you at all. Why are you calling me your son?

I AM NOT HAPPY WITH THIS TRANSACTION!!!!

—Bill

Subject: Now Don't Get All In A Froth
From: SamplesCarLot@gmail.com

Look here Bill, when I call you "son" that just means I like you in a friendly kind of way, that's all. That's the way we do it down here in Georgia. I don't actually think you ARE my son - that would be plum crazy. You see, my real son Verlon came clean out of the womb of his mother (a.k.a. my wife) which you, most certainly, did not. I really don't know why you don't understand me because I speak just as clear as day.

As far as the Chevy goes, I'm afraid there was a minor altercation. As you can see in the snapshot we had a bit of a storm last night and things went all whirly in the car lot, so it looks like she may need some minor adjustments. But don't you worry, with a touch of monkey glue she'll be up and running in no time.

Heck, I'd even be willing to knock off an extra hundred, *but that's just because I like ya!*

I expect to hear from you by tomorrow, otherwise I'm gonna have to let her go to someone else. At this price, she won't last long.

- Jr. Jr.

Subject: Bill?
From: SamplesCarLot@gmail.com

You still there? Now look son, there's no need to get your goose in a lather. I understand you're sore about the Chagrin, but I'll tell you what, I've got a real nice Ford Foible on the lot with your name on it. The u-nuts need to be spliced but it's nothing a little tin spelt and arm sweat won't fix. What do ya say friend?

Your man from the pines - Jr. Samples Jr.

Chapter 9.

Opus Knight

Subject: <u>**Opus Knight**</u>
(Albino, Prophet of the Cosmos)

Conman: <u>**Earl Simplice**</u>
(University Student, Heiress)

Attempted Swindle: <u>**$ 869.50**</u>

Subject: Dearest One…
From: earl_simplice2222@yahoo.com

Greetings to you,

I am really sorry for the suddenness of this message. It's not my wish to get you bothered, but I have no other options. My name is Earl Simplice, I am 23 years old. I live in Durham, where I am at school and I am the only daughter of my parents. My father died last year, but before his death he had willed part of his estate, which amounts to **a Total of GBP 800,000.00** (Eight Hundred Thousand British Pounds) to me.

Now at his death, and because things have become very hard for me (paying my school fees and taking care of my other needs), I made an application to the Security Agency where the money is being deposited for a possible liquidation. I was shocked when they wrote back to say that I will not be able to withdraw the money right now because my father had put a clause on the will, stating that before I will be allowed access to the money I will have to be 25 years old. But I will be given access if I get married before the age of 25 years, in which case, my husband will be legible to liquidate the WILL on my behalf. But today I am only 23 years!

If I can trust you, I will need your assistance in this regard. I will want you to stand in as my own husband. The documents to that effect I shall provide. I will send you the Sole Executor's information so you can contact him and demand the payment of your wife's money to you. I will follow it up from here, providing him with the necessary information or documents. Should you be interested in helping me, please write back to me. I hope that we shall discuss how you want to be remunerated. For my part, I shall be more than willing to part with 20% of the total sum to you.

Please remember that I am writing you this email purely on the ground of trust. While this transaction lasts, we must be able to put emotions aside and not be diverted. Please write back to me if you are interested.

Yours Truly,

Earl Simplice

Subject: Greetings Earl
From: OpusKnight@gmail.com

Dear Miss Simplice,

I'm sorry to hear about your trouble. I've never thought about the commitment of marriage before, especially with a girl named Earl. But if this union could help a soul in need, I would certainly be interested. Can you tell me more?

- Opus Knight

Subject: Thank You For Your Kindest Response
From: earl_simplice2222@yahoo.com

Dear Mr Opus,

I am very delighted to know that you may be interested in being a part of this transaction and it is my hope that everything works out for good.

You are right about the issues of commitment. However, for the purpose of this transaction, I would say that we might not have to get married to get this under way. All I need from you is a confirmation of your genuine interests in helping me claim my inheritance after which we might follow up with anything that develops between us.

I am attaching to this email a picture I took a few weeks ago. In the meantime however, I will need your personal info including where you live, full names, telephone numbers, nationality, age, employment, etc. Thanks once more.

- Simplice Earl

Subject: Yes, I Am *Very* Interested In Helping You
From: OpusKnight@gmail.com

Earl,

Let me begin by saying you are a very beautiful woman. You said you'd like to have some personal information, so allow me to tell you about myself. I am a resident of the great city of New Orleans and a high prophet of The Church of the Cosmos. I have been preaching "cosmic magnetism" for quite a few years now with an increased number of followers. (Just to illustrate how high my cosmic powers are, I've reached level 6 on the magnetic wheel.)

Due to a lack of funds, the Cosmologists and I were using the parking lot of the local bowling alley for our daily service. Unfortunately, we were forced to move because our long hair and magnasuits were found too distracting to the bowlers, so now we're living in City Park. Here's a picture of us at our last group meeting near a bank of elms. I'm in the middle holding our holy orb - The Cosmosphere.

Despite all of our troubles we have big plans for the future and I believe this business deal will help us find a permanent location for our church. In fact, we hope to buy a plot of land within the month.

P.S. I feel very good about your involvement with us Earl. After placing your photograph near The Cosmosphere I sensed a high range of magnetism, particularly in the knee region.

Peace in the cosmos,

Prophet Opus

Subject: You Didnt Answer My Questions!
From: earl_simplice2222@yahoo.com

Dear Prophet Opus,

I am not sure what to say here. Actually, you haven't answered any of the questions I asked in my previous email, and from the looks of things, you are probably looking for believers in your Church. I am a Christian, but not religious and I am not sure I am bound to these things.

The other issues concerning your members and what you do really do not have any impression on me. However, for the purpose of this transaction, I would like to point out that I need someone to help me with the liquidation of my inheritance. If you are interested, why don't you just let me know?

I will ask you again, do you want to go on with this? If so, what are your personal details?

Simplice Earl

Subject: Calm Yourself Child…
From: OpusKnight@gmail.com

Simplice,

In answer to your question, yes, I most certainly *do* want to go through with this. I feel it is divine force that brought you to me. Try not to worry about not being religious. We at The Church of the Cosmos don't judge our fellow humans on such matters. As long as you are trustworthy and reach a magnetic level of 3, we agree to hold our scrutiny. I'm sorry I didn't supply you with the necessary information. Here are the personal details you asked for:

Name: Opus Knight **Age:** 56 **Nationality:** American (of the albino persuasion) **Employment:** Prophet **Address:** Church of The Cosmos (tent in City Park, corner of Harrison Ave. and Lagoon Dr.)
Phone: (504) 545-**** (pay phone, may be out of order)

P.S. Since you were kind enough to send me your picture, I'll send you mine. It hangs over the alter next to our Shrine of the Holy Boot.

I don't mean to scare you, but as you can see, my body exudes magnetism.

Peace and cosmic wellness to you,

- Prophet Opus

Subject: I Need An ID
From: earl_simplice2222@yahoo.com

Prophet Opus,

I am not scared. But I want to ask you something. Do you agree with the arrangements as I spelt them out in my first email to you? Are you dealing with me as a person or as a leader of a church? You seem to be spotless and holy as far as I can see, but I will need you to send me a form of ID.

I will be forwarding to you the attorneys contact information so you may contact him. But I have one worry; he might want to know or see evidence of our relationship since it was spelt out in the WILL that only my husband could assist me in applying for and collecting the funds and we are not really married.

I would need your permission to apply for a marriage certificate to provide to the attorney by way of authenticating our union. I want you to know it might cost money.

Simplice Earl.

Subject: You Have My Permission
From: OpusKnight@gmail.com

Dearest Earl - Child of The Cosmos,

Yes, go ahead and apply for the certificate. After alerting the Cosmologists in a meeting last night they came to understand our relationship will in no way effect the church, so they fully endorse this holy marriage.

Don't worry about the license fees, as your husband, I will take care of all expenses, including a full cosmic wedding with flowers and a Silver Cone of Knowledge. I was able to secure the "leisure room" at Mid-City Lanes. Their only stipulation is that we wear bowling shoes and don't hog the ball polisher. Which reminds me, will you require a honeymoon? I know a nice place in Chalmette that has a complimentary pancake breakfast.

P.S. Just to warn you, my energy core has been logged "high" so you should plan accordingly. Let us pray for a speedy union.

-The Prophet

Subject: Get This Clear In Your Head!
From: earl_simplice2222@yahoo.com

Prophet,

Look, I am not going to have sex with you! I only need this relationship because I need my funds released sooner than the stipulation of the WILL letter. I don't know why you said "holy marriage" and you were sarcastic with the mention of a honeymoon. I think I have told you what I want from you. I asked you a simple something and yet you keep rigmaroling!

I would like to make a point clear here. This inheritance is all I've got and I am very serious about this business. I am not a believer in your doctrine so I take excemption to your addressing me as a "Child of The Cosmos" or whatever you call it. I am sorry if I am being rude, but you need to know the line between what I have discussed with you and the church or your faith.

I need to see an ID of you. And since you mentioned you could take care of all expenses, and in order to ensure that we are able to prove our union, I was able to meet with a clerk who worked at a marriage magestrate here and he is willing to help arrange a marriage licence at a cost. In fact, he is asking for the sum of **450 pounds**. I would have paid it myself, but I am short of money right now.

In addition I need a scanned copy of your ID, which is for my assurance. After you send the money, send me the payment confirmation information that you will be issued at the Western Union money transfer centre.

This is the information:

Mr Desmond Hill - Session House - Highfield Road Dartford, Kent DA1 2JW England.

Please get it done!

Subject: From The Prophet…
From: OpusKnight@gmail.com

Earl, I can assure you I am just as serious as you are and I would never consider flagrant sex acts or rigamarolery of any kind. I really hope you stop all of this negative thinking and warm up to me. I'm sure once you feel the power of my auras you'll change your tune (after all, I have 6 in my left thigh alone!).

I've included my church ID card as you requested.

Church Of The Cosmos
Member ID Card

License Number: G-450-299-41-0

Opus K. Knight
333 Lagoon Dr.
New Orleans, LA 70301

Level:
Cosmic AAA

Birth Date: Sex: Restrictions:
2-22-51   M   Corrective Left Eye,
                Hypomelanosis

Signature: *O. Knight*   Issued: Expires: Magnetism:
                         4-23-07   2-22-11   Very High

Subject: Send The Payment Information!!!
From: earl_simplice2222@yahoo.com

Opus,

I acknowledge the receipt of the ID you sent. For the umpteen time you must understand that we are doing all of this only for the purpose of claiming my inheritance from the agency! While not boasting of being a virgin, I wasn't expecting you to make comments about sexual things, but it is OK.

I believe by now you should have sent the 450 pounds to Mr. Desmond Hill, as I had told you? Here is his phone number in case you feel like calling him. +447045703723.

Waiting to hear from you…

- Earl

Subject: Fear Not, I Have Consulted The Boot…
From: OpusKnight@gmail.com

Dearest Earl,

To get the money for the marriage license I'm afraid I'll need to dip into the church coffers. 480 pounds comes to $869.50 U.S. dollars and we spent much of our reserve last month repairing the chrome plating on The Cosmosphere. I'm not sure how we'll get it, but have no fear, I prayed to the Shrine of The Holy Boot which you see here in this glorious photo.

Earl, this boot has shown me guidance through many a troubling time. It belonged to Erasmus T. Manfur, a horse-breeder by trade and the founder of Cosmic Magnetism. It was the only thing remaining after he was struck by a bolt of lightning while impregnating a filly back in 1882. Whenever we are in need of spiritual guidance we turn to its great powers of insight and reason. (Happily, the boot finds our situation favorable.)

Hoping your polarity is positive,

Prophet Opus

Subject: Ok
From: earl_simplice2222@yahoo.com

Whatever you say Prophet…

Subject: Question…
From: OpusKnight@gmail.com

Child,

I was wondering, do you know of any plots of land for sale? We are looking to buy a large parcel with a favorable longitude for our new church. Perhaps there's something in your area? (Please note - it must be sunny and have direct access to the Galactic Core.)

- O.

Subject: Just Get It Done!
From: earl_simplice2222@yahoo.com

Look, I don't remember telling you I was an estate agent. I told you that you were being sarcastic the last time, yet you denied it, and now you are making a derisive statement!

We have wasted enough time doing nothing. You have been rigmaroling. You have said time and again that you have the money for the license, yet you won't send it. Instead you keep asking me questions you ought not to.

I will say here and now that if you feel you don't want to go on, please be bold enough to tell me. But if you do want to go on, then you will send the money and forward me the payment confirmation information so we may make progress!

-Simplice

Subject: Don't You Get Testy With Me Child!
From: OpusKnight@gmail.com

HOW DARE YOU TALK TO ME LIKE THAT! DON'T YOU KNOW I AM A HIGH PROPHET OF THE COSMOS? DON'T YOU KNOW I'VE CHANNELED THE ENERGIES OF ERASMUS T. MANFUR AND LIVED TO TELL ABOUT IT? DON'T YOU KNOW I AM KEEPER OF THE HOLY BOOT?

Now look here girl, you have been testy with me from the start, but I'm afraid you've gone too far this time! I am *not* sarcastic. I am *not* derisive. And I certainly am not a *rigamaroler!* I was simply asking if you know of any land for sale where we could begin building our church. We are in desperate need of sheltering The Cosmosphere since the damp New Orleans air is beginning to diminish the outer confabulatory layer.

Oh, I will get you your $869.50 for this so-called marriage license Earl, but you've got to cease being so hostile! All of this negative energy is throwing off my inner magnetism and causing unrest in the church. I've already had two members drop out and one has filed a formal complaint with city officials! Truthfully, I'm starting to have doubts about you and not just because you're a "non-virgin," as you have said. As a prophet, I must insist you be kind and courteous to me from now on. If we can't conclude this business deal in a civilized way, I'll just have to get funding somewhere else.

Speaking of which, I just received an email from a very nice fellow in Nigeria with a business proposal that promises to bring the Cosmologists quite a lot of wealth. *Now what do you think of that?!!*

Subject: So Sorry, Please Forgive Me
From: earl_simplice2222@yahoo.com

Dear Mr Opus,

Please accept my heartfelt sincere apologies for the way I wrote to you. I am so sorry, kindly forgive me. But I really don't have any idea where you can get land.

You mentioned you just received an email from a very nice fellow in Nigeria. Please Prophet, be careful of Nigerians, THEY ARE ALL FRAUDSTERS.

In regards to our own transaction, dont think that I am talking to you rudely, cos all I am really after is for us to complete the transaction so that you can get your % and use it to build your church.

I put in my daily prayers for you Prophet, so just try and make sure you send the money to the clerk, okay.

I await to hear from you soon.

Subject: That's Better…
From: OpusKnight@gmail.com

Dear Earl,

Well, I won't lie. I'm still stinging a little from being called a rigamaroler, but as the great Manfur would say, "All is forgiven in the black swirl of the cosmos."

As far as the money is concerned, I'm working diligently on that. I have the Cosmologists out on the street selling incense, body oils and my very own invention, the "Magnaboot." It's footwear I crafted myself that provides direct contact with magnets lying at the Earth's core. (Their effectiveness lie in the steel insoles which greatly invigorate the contrivatory system.) So far, we've sold only one pair but the patchouli oil more than makes up for it.

Oh, I've got some good news! You can forget about looking for land because we seem to have lucked into a very nice real estate deal. That African fellow I told you about says he's going to sell us a plot of land for an extremely low price. It's apparently on a lovely grassy knoll right on the edge of a diamond mine. (This is perfect for The Cosmosphere considering it runs on crystal power.)

The fellow's name is "Charles Taylor" and he says the government is trying to liquidate all of his assets on account of a "squirrelous plot against his innate character." He said he would rather sell it to "a prophet of a God-fearing persuasion" rather than his detractors who wish him "utmost harm to his personal being." It all seems to be on the up and up - he sent me a certificate and everything!

Keep yourself magnetized,

Opus

Subject: Thanks A lot For Your Acceptance, But Please Be Warned
From: earl_simplice2222@yahoo.com

Dear Mr Opus,

Thanks for getting back to me as well as for the appologies accepted. I am really so sorry.

Please Prophet, dont deal with anybody from Nigeria. They are not trustworthy and they will fraud you. Please stay away from the offer, it is not legit.

Subject: Fraud?
From: OpusKnight@gmail.com

Dear child, I appreciate your concern, but I honestly think this Charles Taylor fellow is legitimate. He said he received my email address "from a divine source directly from God" and also from "an advanced computing system from the Bank of Liberia." He says this diamond mine was one of the best in the country. He included a photo of it just so I would know how many shovels to bring.

I must say, the Cosmologists would do very well building a settlement on its perimeter. In the morning they could dig for diamonds to sell in town, and in the afternoon they could commune with the cosmos. He's only asking $500 for the deed and I could easily earn that with just three Mangnaboot sales!

Do you really think he's trying to con me? How could a man so polite and earnest be a criminal? After all, if this deal is legitimate, we could spend our boot money on that mine and really establish a place for our new church. In fact, Wendell, one of my top earners, is out on Canal Street today so we should have enough money to complete the deal by sundown.

I want to thank you for looking out for us Earl, you're a good girl. And because of your warning, I will wrap myself in a cloak of magnetism and consult The Cone of Knowledge.

-The Prophet

Subject: Extremely Urgent!!!!!!!!
From: earl_simplice2222@yahoo.com

Dear Mr Opus,

I got your message, but I still have to warn you to be careful. But whats going on with our deal? I met with the clerk yesterday and I told him to be patient.

Please Prophet, I really want us to get things done. Make a fast move because I am seriously down over here!

Simplice

Subject: Confused
From: OpusKnight@gmail.com

Earl,

I've been thinking. If this Taylor fellow is a fraud, how do I know you're not a fraud too? After all, your emails are somewhat similar.

I am really very confused right now and I'm not sure what to do. Perhaps if you and I solidified our relationship I'd feel more secure. Maybe we *should* get married and live like man and wife. I could run the church and you could run the commune, and maybe eventually we could start up an intergalactic globular cluster of our own.

As a prophet, I should receive a divine sign, but never before have I been so confused. Do I give my money to you and get married, or do I give it to Charles Taylor and become a diamond miner? This indecisiveness is so upsetting it's throwing my magnetism askew. There's only one thing to do - I must pull myself together and consult The Boot!

P.S. On another note, those Magnaboots really seem to be taking off. Wendell made a big sale to a busload of Swedish nuns yesterday, so we now have more than enough money to cover costs for the marriage license and even a full cosmic wedding if need be. If those boots continue to sell this well, we will have more money than we know what to do with.

Be restful my child.

- Prophet O.

Subject: You Are Wasting Time!
From: earl_simplice2222@yahoo.com

Somehow, I do not know what to say. I have told you before to keep me out of your church and stop calling me your child!

What we have here is a working relationship. You are a man of age and I am not in the best position to advise you about what you do with your time and money. And please stop telling me about Wendell!

I must know where we stand. It's of absolute importance that you let me know if I should look else where for assistance. You seem to be playing for time or something.

I want to have an answer from you today because I am tired of being kept in suspense!

Simplice

Subject: Prove It To Me!
From: OpusKnight@gmail.com

Earl,

I've told you countless times I am a Prophet of The Cosmos and I represent mental magnetism of the highest order. How dare you snap at me that way! I take offense to all of your accusations, and just so you know, Wendell is one of the church's most esteemed members. He has quickly risen to level 4 on the magnetic wheel in just three short weeks!

I understand how much this inheritance means to you, but it seems now you just want my money. How do I know I can trust you? This Charles Taylor fellow that you accuse of being "a fraudster" has just sent me a picture of himself swearing to God that he is a man of honor that can be trusted. Do *you* have a picture of yourself swearing to God? Well…*do you???*

Earl, I have $1,000 of Magnaboot money sitting right here next to me. Send me proof that you are as honest as Charles Taylor and I swear on the bosom of Manfur I will deliver the money to you today!

-Your Prophet

Subject: Ok, I've Had Enough
From: earl_simplice2222@yahoo.com

Prophet,

Go ahead and send your money to Charles Taylor since he has sworn to God!

Subject: Thanks For The Advice
From: OpusKnight@gmail.com

Dearest Simplice,

The Cosmologists and I have decided to take your advice and buy Charles Taylor's diamond mine since you said "go ahead since he has sworn to God." I sent him $500 for the land and he immediately sent me this map of its location in central Liberia.

It's a little vague, but he said it will all make sense once we get there. He's really a very kind man Earl. He's promised to take us directly to the mouth of the mine in a black Rolls Royce. He said if we dug every day from morning til night we would be "up to our necks in diamonds" *and* we'll be able to drink from a "river of gold." It looks like the Cosmologists and I are finally going to do all right for ourselves.

I just want you to know you are always welcome to come and join us in Africa if you'd like - that marriage invitation is still open. I may be an older man, but my magnetism is still very high, at least that's what The Boot says, and it's never wrong.

Keep in touch Earl. May you be at peace in the dewy folds of the cosmos.

Your Prophet - Opus Knight

Chapter 10.

Steve Teufelman

Subject: <u>Steve Teufelman</u>
   (Collector of "trunks of treasures")

Con Men: <u>Shadak Sheriff</u>
   (Dying man who "has not lived his life so well")

   <u>Dr. Smith Clifford</u>
   (Operations Manager - Abudanza Security)

Attempted Swindle: <u>Undetermined Amount,</u>
   <u>Possible Identity Theft</u>

Subject: PLEASE HELP
From: shadak1@yahoo.com.ph

Dear Sir,

Can a dieing man trust you with a huge sum of money to help him carry out his last wish? Reply to me urgently to get more details.

Subject: Yeah, Ok…
From: TheTeufelMan@gmail.com

Hey dying man,

I think I could help with your last wish. Does it involve anything messy? I don't like messy.

- Steve

Subject: Greetings To You My Friend
From: shadak1@yahoo.com.ph

Dear Steve,

Thanks for you swift response. As you read this, I don't want you to feel sorry for me because I believe everyone will die someday. My name is SHADAK SHERIFF a merchant in Dubai. I have been diagnosed with esophageal cancer which has already spread into the stomach and intestines. It has defiled all forms of medical treatment and right now I have only a few months to live according to medical experts.

I have not particularly lived my life so well as I never really cared for anyone, not even myself. Though I am very rich, I was never generous. I was always hostile to people and only focused on my business. But now I regret all this as I now know there is more to life than just wanting to have made all the money in the world.

I believe when God gives me a second chance to come to this world, I would live my life a different way. I want God to be merciful to me and accept my soul so I have decided to give alms to charity organizations, as I want this to be one of the last good deeds I do on earth.

So far I have distributed money to some charity organizations but now that my health has deteriorated so badly, I cannot do this myself anymore. I once asked members of my family to distribute the money but they refused and kept it to themselves. Hence, I do not trust them anymore.

The last of my money, which no one knows of, is the huge cash deposit of **$18 million dollars** that I have with a finance company abroad. I will want you to help me go there and collect this deposit and dispatch it to charity organizations. **I have set aside 10% for you and your time.**

Please get back to me as soon as possible so that I can furnish you with the relevant documents. Best regards as I wait your quick response. God be with you.

SHADAK SHERRIF

Subject: Ok, whatever…
From: TheTeufelMan@gmail.com

Sheriff,

Yeah, you're right, everyone does die someday. That's what I keep telling people, but they never listen.

I think maybe I could help you out with this thing because I could really use that kind of cash. I'm a little low and if I don't get next month's rent money those voices in my head are going to start telling me to do stuff again and I'm running out of places to dig.

- Steve

Subject: Thanks For Your Help
From: shadak1@yahoo.com.ph

Dear Friend,

Thanks for your concern. In my last email to you I introduced myself and gave you a summary of the present predicament I have found myself in. I felt that after our initial communication I should be able to determine if we can precede based on certain intuitive feelings.

If you would be able to help me fulfill this last living request of passing on a privately kept fund of **$18,000,000,00**, I would need you to get back to me on the following issues:

1. That you are a GOD FEARING person and are in a position to be trusted with such a large amount of funds and that you have a heart for charity and thus would not have any problems locating the right human aid groups to disburse the fund to.

2. That you are willing to contact the finance company holding the deposit to discuss the terms of releasing the funds to you.

3. That you fully understand this transaction up to this stage and you are ready to proceed under these terms.

4. How old are you and do you have a family?

5. Please send your full contact details, full names, phone and fax numbers as well as your address.

I will need to send your contact details to the finance company regarding the release of these funds. (Note, I can not sit too long on my system becose of my condidtion, so I can not chat with you, I am very sorry.) I await further communication.

Yours Faithfully – Shadak Sherrif

Subject: Fine…
From: TheTeufelMan@gmail.com

Hey Sheriff,

Yeah, I already said I'd help. Didn't I already tell you my name is Steve and I live at 378 Elm St. in Pit Falls? I'm about 30 and I don't really have a family anymore, not after the accident anyway.

- Steve

Subject: Please Provide Proper Informations
From: shadak1@yahoo.com.ph

Dear Steve,

I got your mail, the informations you provided will be insufficient for the documentations.

You are required to provide me with your full names, age, complete address and telephone number. I will like you to know what next to do as soon as I get this information from you.

Regards,

Shadak

Subject: Ok already…jeez
From: TheTeufelMan@gmail.com

Hey Shadak,

I don't know why you're yelling at me. Yelling isn't going to help anything. You need to learn to be nicer to people. Bad things happen to people who aren't nice, just ask my neighbor Wendy Kleinpaste.

Anyway, I said I'll help and I mean it. I'll disburse your funds for you real good, there's no problem there. I've already told you about a million times my address is 378 Elm St. in Ohio and my name is Steve Teufelman. Sometimes I go by the name Screech – but that's mostly after midnight when the owls come out. My phone number is 487-9336. But whatever you do, don't call after 1 a.m., that's my special time.

P.S. Hey, Sherrif, you got a girlfriend? I used to, but she started asking too many questions.

Screech

Subject: Pix Attached
From: shadak1@yahoo.com.ph

Dear Screech,

Thanks for your response. I would want you to take this transaction very serious because my situation here in the hospital is very bad.

I will attach to this email the certificate of deposit from a security and finance company and my pictures in the hospital.

I got this fund as a result of contracts I did with Yukos oil. This fund is deposited in two trunk boxes and is presently with the security company in Amsterdam The Netherlands. I deposited the funds as personal effects & family treasures.

I cannot call you on phone for now because of my present situation but I can manage to type email. I will like you to contact the security company now so that they can tell you how you will collect the trunks.

ABUDANZA SECURITIES SERVICES COMPANY BV,
TEL # 0031-610-149-147 FAX: +31-847-302-818
E-mail: abudan.zansec@europe.com

I will also like you to go to Amsterdam yourself to collect the trunks so that I can be rest assured that every thing is ok. I put all my trust in you. I have asked the lawyer in the hospital to prepare a power of attoney for you so that you can have a legal backing. I will be expecting to hear from you as soon so we can proceed with the transaction.

Yours faithfully,

Shadak Sheriff

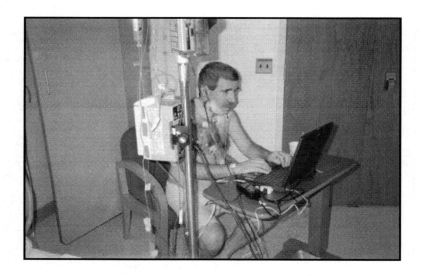

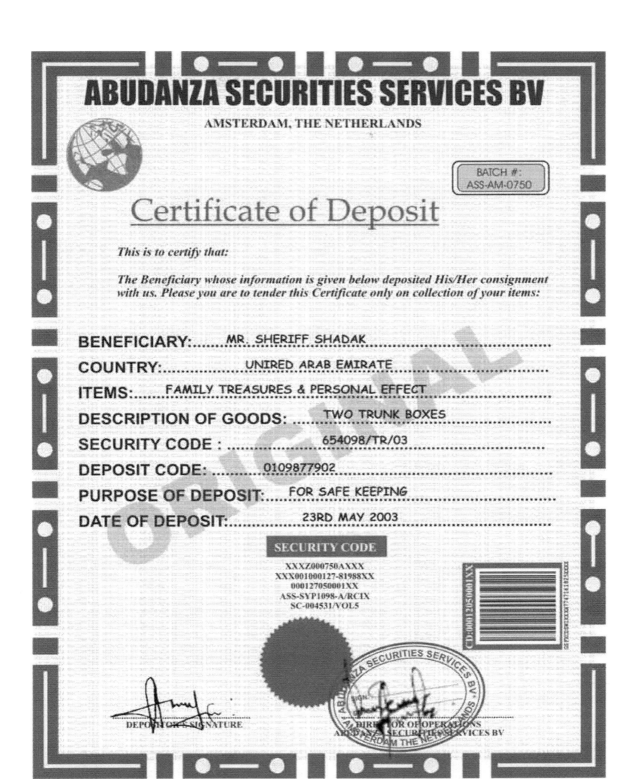

Subject: I don't know…
From: TheTeufelMan@gmail.com

Hey Sheriff,

Man, you're not looking so good. I gotta tell you, whatever they're doing to you in the hospital isn't good. I'd lay off the morphine drip for a while.

Look, I don't know if I can go all the way to Amsterdam right now, I got some pretty important stuff to take care of here at the house. I had some trouble last night and now I've got a real mess on my hands. It's the kind of mess that bleach just won't clean up, if you know what I mean.

P.S. Hey, what kind of girls do they have in Amsterdam? If I get in my car at 2 a.m., how long will it take me to get there?

Screech

Subject: CONTACT SECURITY COMPANY
From: shadak1@yahoo.com.ph

Dear Friend,

I dont know how long it will take you to get there, but you can contact the security company to confirm that.

Shadak

Subject: I'm The Guy Who's Gonna Help Out Sheriff
From: TheTeufelMan@gmail.com

Abudanza Security Service,

I'm a friend of Shadak Sheriff and we've got this deal worked out where I'm going to take care of some trunks for him. I've already told him I'm on board with this whole thing because I really need the money. I'm building an entertainment center down in my basement which is requiring lots of expensive pit digging and chains, so that dough is really gonna come in handy. Let me know what I gotta do to get that treasure a.s.a.p.

- Steve Teufelman

Subject: Consignment Notification
From: abudan.zansec@europe.com

ABUDANZA SECURITY & FINANCE COMPANY

Dear Sir.

We write to confirm that the deposit of Mr. Shadak Sheriff is in our custody, be informed that you will be required as the beneficiary of the deposit of Mr. Shadaks two trunk boxes.

You are requested to provide this office with the following requirements and documents to ensure that you are the sole beneficiary of the deposited boxes declared to us as **FAMILY TREASURES** so that the said deposit can be released to you.

Ensure to send to us the requested documents and proof of identification for record and safety reasons.

1. A valid proof of identification (passport or drivers license).
2. Copy of the certificate of deposit and power of Attorney.
3. A copy of the change of beneficiary.
4. Telephone and fax number.
5. We require to know your age.
6. State your contact address and phone numbers.

We also want to inform you that there are some **CHARGES OF CUSTOM AND CLEARING** which are needed to be paid before we release your consignment of two trunk boxes deposited with us. However, for now we can't tell you the total cost, we have to contact the Accounting Department to put the total sum together and then we will get back to you as soon as we have the actual cost of the charges.

Best Regards,

Dr. Smith Clifford - Operations Manager

Subject: Yeah yeah, I got it already
From: TheTeufelMan@gmail.com

Hey Abudanza,

All this information you're asking for I already gave Sheriff about a billion times, so why don't you just ask him for it? I'll try to find my driver's license but I haven't seen it around for a few weeks. In fact, it's been missing ever since I took Brenda for a drive to the woods.

Here's a picture of her wearing a dress with flowers. It's not my fault what happened, she knew how I felt about pink begonias.

P.S. Hey, what kind of "treasures" does Sheriff's family have anyway? Are there any gold teeth?

- Steve

Subject: I found it!
From: TheTeufelMan@gmail.com

Hey Abudanza,

I finally found my driver's license. It was right where I dropped it next to a big cedar log out in the forest. I had to wash it off because it was covered in a lot of mud and other sticky stuff, so it's kind of drying out right now on the radiator.

I just want you to know I'm still completely ready to help Sheriff out. I've helped out a lot of people over the years - like Sharon Mincemeyer.

Tell Sheriff I'm coming to Amsterdam to see him. I hope those trunks fit in the trunk of my car, it is pretty big after all. Hey, they aren't oozing anything are they? If so, I can always bring the plastic sheeting.

-Steve

Subject: Consignment Notification
From: abudan.zansec@europe.com

Plaease do not contact this office anymore! We don't deal with woodlocks like you! We have aleady informed Shadak Sheriff.

-Dr Smith Clifford (Operations Manager - Abudanza)

Subject: WHAT!!!!!!!!!!!!
From: TheTeufelMan@gmail.com

Hey Doctor,

Look, don't you go calling me a woodlock. If anything, you're the woodlock around here. You're a trillion times more woodlocky than I could ever be. In fact, when I look up woodlock in the dictionary, I see your woodlocked face!

Personally, I don't think you were ever going to give me the trunks of treasure in the first place. This makes me very angry. Believe me, you don't want me angry. The voice is telling me to find my special gloves…and the clam knife.

- Screech "not a woodlock" Teufelman

Subject: Ah Jeez, I'm sorry…
From: TheTeufelMan@gmail.com

Hey man, I'm really sorry I freaked out on the security company like that. I didn't mean to, it's just that they were asking all of these really complicated questions and I already gave them the information they wanted about a zillion times. So to make it up to you, I'm gonna get in my car and drive to Amsterdam to help you out. I know those trunks of treasure are really getting on your nerves. I found a map in the back seat of my mother's car and I think I can be there sometime tomorrow if I don't stop for anything like gas or parking lot attendants.

So what do you say? Can we be friends again? Hey, do you like jewelry? I've got a ton of it in the glove compartment – necklaces, bracelets, hair combs, whatever you want. How about a nice ring, like this one? Girls like rings, especially if you rinse them off first.

-Steve

Subject: You Must Be Right
From: shadak1@yahoo.com.ph

Dear Sir,

The security company told me that you are not worthy to handle my treasures the way you sounded.

You have the chance to prove me wrong. I am still your friend, as long as you play to the rule.

-Shadak

Subject: No Problem Man
From: TheTeufelMan@gmail.com

Hey, thanks for listening to me man, it's really good to have you back. Like I said, I'm gonna jump in my car and hightail it on over there. I gotta tell you though, I'm not sure about those Abudanza guys, they sound like trouble to me. If they said I'm not worthy, they got another thing coming. They also think I'm a woodlock and I told them about a gazillion times I'm not. If you want me to take any of them out, I will, that's no problem. Just like you said, I'm going to "play to the rule."

Hey Shadak, do you know what exit I take to get to Amsterdam?

-Steve

Subject: Hey Man, You Gotta Help Me Out…
From: TheTeufelMan@gmail.com

Shadak man,

Look, I'm out on the road here and I think I missed my exit. My map said to take the turnpike past Buffalo then keep going straight, but things are starting to look really weird. I don't like it here Shadak. The voice said I should just keep heading north, but the last time I did that I ended up with a bag of fingers on the dashboard. Maybe I'll head east.

-Steve

Subject: Ok…here's the thing
From: TheTeufelMan@gmail.com

Look, I know you were really wanting me to pick up that treasure for you, but I got a little side-tracked by this girl Rhonda….

It turns out she knows where all the best incinerators are in town, plus, she's really good with piano wire. So if you don't mind, I think I'll just stay here for a while.

Hey, when you move those trunks, don't forget to lift with your knees. Oh…and don't forget the duct tape.

Your friend,

Screech

Chapter 11.

Norman Dodd

Subject: Norman Dodd
    (Ventriloquist, Inheritor)

Con Men: Raymond Williams
    (Attorney for the Late Michael Dodd
     and Manager of "The Will")
    Mr. Brick
    (Probate Officer)

Attempted Swindle: $8,819.56

Subject: Good Day
From: unionattorney_chamber01@yahoo.com

Dear Friend,

The Trustees and Executors to the Will of our late client wish to notify you that you were listed as a beneficiary to the total sum of **9,900, 000.00 GBP** (Nine million nine hundred thousand British pounds) in the Codicil and Last Testament of the deceased.

Let me try to explain to you first hand the details of this inheritance because it is important that you understand why you have been contacted in the first instance.

The case of our client is an unsual one as his death was abrupt and without a will covering this sum mentioned to you. This leaves us no choice but to appoint an inheritor. Rather than allow these funds to be confiscated, I need a very reputable person to be nominated as the beneficiary outside the United Kingdom.

I am contacting you because you bear the same surname as our late client. Because of this, I can easily file for the sum to be released to your account as the inheritor.

It is important for me to know of your interest in this matter, especially when you only got my email on the internet. But bear it in mind emphatically that you are being contacted for something legitimate.

In your acceptance of this deal, we request that you kindly forward a current photo, a telephone number and forwarding address to enable us to file necessary documents at our High Court Probate Division for the release of this sum of money to you.

Please note that I will demand maximum confidentiality and discreteness in all matters.

Congratulations, I await your early response.

Attorney Raymond Williams { ESQ}
Union Attorney Chamber

Subject: I'm Getting an Inheritance?
From: TheHandsMan@gmail.com

Mr. Williams,

I must say I'm thrilled by this announcement, but I'm a little surprised. I had no idea a person could inherit such a large amount just because of their last name. But I'm not complaining, that kind of money will sure be welcome right now. And don't worry, I promise I'll keep this "discreet," like you said. I won't even tell mother, and she knows *everything*.

You asked for a current photo, so here's one of me and my business partner, "Chippy."

We perform a ventriloquism act called "Dodd and the Magic Hand" three nights a week at Club Titters on Rampart Street.

If I do say so, it's one of the best shows in the French Quarter. We've got a lot of classic gags like "The Drunken Spaniard," "Hide The Peanut," and "The Triple Kitten Toss." Chippy also does a great Mike Douglas impression.

I've included the information you requested below. Please let me know what I need to do next, Chippy is getting quite anxious.

Mr. Norman Dodd
1010 Rue Dumaine
New Orleans, LA 70116

Subject: Death Certificate
From: unionattorney_chamber01@yahoo.com

Dear Norman,

Thank you for your brief email response. I have already done the most necessary thing to make your funds transfered to you. Please note I have sent you a DEATH CERTIFICATE and a photograph of our late client MICHEAL DODD. Please, you are to keep it safely in case anyone asks you to present it to show you are the real beneficiary.

Now I want you to contact Mr. Bricks at the probate office yourself. Say you want to make a registration of your inheritance so you can recieve a "letter of guarantee" without any interferance. Here is the email address
probateofficeregistr@myway.com

Best regards.

Raymond Williams "ESQ"

HENDRIX HOSPITAL
5 Craig Boulevard, Manchester, M14 9EZ

DEATH CERTIFICATE

I HEREBY CERTIFY that I have medically attended to

MICHEAL DODD

Of **16 CONNAUGHT TERRACE HOVE, EAST SUSSEX** who was apparently or stated to be aged **68** years. I last saw **HIM** on the **8TH JANUARY, 2004** was then suffering from **COMPLICATED CAUSES**

Died as I am aware, or informed on the **9TH** day of **JANUARY** at **HENDRIX HOSPITAL** And that the cause of death was to the best of my knowledge and belief as herein stated.

Viz **EXCESSIVE BLEEDING ON ADMISSION**

Primary Cause **INTERNAL BLEEDING**

Secondary Cause **MULTIPLE FRACTURE**

And that the deceased had continued **BLEEDING**

UNTIL DEATH

Witnessed my hands this **10TH** day **JANUARY, 2004**

Medical Director

1. State address   2. Omit "apparently or" state to be "as the cause may be"
3. Omit "aware or when hour of death is known from report   4. State the time
5. State duration of illness if possible

NOTE: that by primary cause of death is meant the disease present at the time, which initiated the train of events leading there to and not a secondary contributory or immediate cause terminal condition or mode of death.

Subject: Ok!
From: TheHandsMan@gmail.com

Mr. Williams,

Thanks for sending the photo and death certificate, I'll make sure and keep them safe. In fact, I'll hide them in my special place under the mattress. Only Chippy knows about it and he only goes there when he wants to play with one of my Shirley Temple dolls.

P.S. I'm sorry to hear Mr. Dodd died from "complicated causes." Chippy was wondering if he bled to death because his doctor was "on the sauce."

- Norman Dodd

Subject: You Must Get Things Moving Now
From: unionattorney_chamber01@yahoo.com

The excessive bleeding occurred after he had a major surgical operation when he had an auto accident on his way to a friends birthday party, which he could not survive.

Mr. Norman, how far have you gone with the probate registration? You must really get things moving now and do remember to always keep me abreast.

- Raymond Williams

Subject: A Little Trouble Here
From: TheHandsMan@gmail.com

Mr. Williams,

I contacted Mr. Bricks at the probate office and told him we need that letter of guarantee, but he said I owe him 4,520 pounds for an official stamp - that comes to $8,819.56 US dollars! I don't know how we're going to get that much money because the truth is Chippy got us into some real hot water yesterday.

I'm not sure what happened, but during the matinee he socked an audience member right in the nose. All she did was ask what kind of handkerchief he was made of, but I guess that was enough to set him off. As you can imagine Mr. Ernie the club owner was furious. He said he'll give us one more chance, but if we don't sell 200 tickets tomorrow night he's going to replace us with our competition "Paco and Kornfly." These two charlatans stole our flaming chihuahua act years ago and they've been raking it in every since.

Here's their publicity photo. Don't let the slick good looks fool you, evil emanates from every pore. Mr. Williams, believe me, if we're replaced by this sinister duo, our career will be over. (Some say Kornfly has a secret compartment in his chest for killer bees.)

P.S. Chippy was wondering if we could get an advance on the inheritance money.

He says he needs a new suit and a steak dinner after the stress of his "altercation." I know it's a lot to ask, but he's being quite insistent.

Yours in haste…Norman

Subject: Urgent!
From: unionattorney_chamber01@yahoo.com

Norman,

I am in reciept of your mail concerning your family issues. Always listen to my advice, you should not let this inheritance money INTOXICATE you. You must learn to keep your mouth shot.

And Norman, you must pay the probate to enable them to stamp your document. Do notice if they don`t receive your payment soon you will not get your inheritance at all.

I HOPE YOU KNOW THAT.

- Raymond Williams

Subject: Don't Worry, We Have A Plan…
From: TheHandsMan@gmail.com

Mr. Williams,

First of all, I am not intoxicated. Second of all, in no way are Paco and Kornfly my "family." They are evil puppeteers who will stop at nothing to put Chippy and I out of business.

Ok, ok, I know I need to pay the probate, but when I asked Mr. Ernie how much money we brought in during our big Saturday show he said it was "less than a three-legged pony ride on Christmas eve." Which I guess means not much. (Frankly, I don't understand this considering the entire Ladies Club was there and Chippy only used the "c" word once.) So the bad news is, we don't have enough money to pay the registration fee *and* we got fired to boot.

But I don't want you to be discouraged because we've got a very good idea how to get that money. Listen to this…Chippy heard from a reliable source that Paco is an illegal alien. And if I'm not mistaken, illegal aliens aren't allowed to perform ventriloquism on American soil no matter how many double-knit suits they own. So here's the plan - when Paco and Kornfly go on stage tonight, we'll slip an anonymous note under their dressing room door demanding the money - otherwise we're spilling the beans to Mr. Ernie.

So give us one night Mr. Williams and we'll have a tall stack of money for you, and believe me, they won't be pesos either!

-Dodd

Subject: MR BRICKS IS WAITING!!!!!
From: unionattorney_chamber01@yahoo.com

Dear Dodd,

I have recieved the mail that you sent trying to explain the delay and I quietly understand your point. But please notice that if the probate office does not recieve your money by tomorrow, they will not be happy.

You must write to him immediately!

- Mr Williams

Subject: Grettings Probate, It's Norman Dodd Again
From: TheHandsMan@gmail.com

Mr. Bricks,

I'm sorry for the delay, but after writing a very successful letter to some "business associates," Chippy and I now have the money for the registration fee. Although our attorney keeps insisting we send it to you as soon as possible, Chippy is having second thoughts. He thinks you're charging too much for the stamp. After all, in America a stamp only costs 44 cents!

- Norman Dodd

Subject: From Probate
From: probateregistr@myway.com

Attention: Dodd

Norman, we are not begging you to send the money, the choice is yours. But you are offending us by not sending it. That means you are a fool and you don`t know how to appreciate a good thing.

Even though you are the real beneficiary of the funds, we will be happy if your attorney declines from this very transaction. You do not know what Mr. Williams is going through. I wish you were here so you could feel for him.

One thing is certain, if I were in his position, I would have let your inheritance be consficated **BECAUSE YOU ARE NOT RELIABLE!**

- Mr Bricks

Subject: Ok, Now I Am Very Upset
From: TheHandsMan@gmail.com

Mr. Williams,

I want you to know Chippy and I wrote to Mr. Bricks and told him we have the money for the registration form, but all he did was yell at us and call us fools! I don't know why he has to be so mean because we're doing the best we can. He really hurt our feelings, isn't that right Chippy?

"How many times do I gotta tell 'ya Dodd, the man's a jackass…"

"Chippy! Watch your mouth!" I want you to know Chippy doesn't yell at people for fun, he just has some anger issues. If you don't believe me, just ask Mother.

Listen Mr. Williams, could you please talk some sense into Mr. Bricks. I have the money, but I'm not going to give it to him until he apologizes.

Your friend,

Norman

Subject: Everything Is Going To Be Fine
From: unionattorney_chamber01@yahoo.com

Dear Norman,

How are you doing with Chippy and your lovely Mother? How are Chippy's feelings?   I hope you are all doing better?

I got your mail saying the probate office yelled at you. Norman, I don't think he is trying to hurt you. Mr. Bricks is not a "jackass" and he is not trying to coerce with you. One thing you should know, Bricks is a friendly human being and even though he did not apologized to you, I am tendering an apology on his behalf okay? So Norman, "I am sorry".

I think I adviced you before that you will have to send him the payment this very day. But make sure you are calm and friendly so everything goes successful ok?

- Raymond Williams "Esq"

Subject: NO MORE PANSYING AROUND, SEE?!!
From: TheHandsMan@gmail.com

"Look Williams, Dodd isn't available to talk right now on account of a little run in with Mother so you're dealing directly with Chippy now. In fact, I'm taking care of all of the business from now on.   Not only do I not want any guff from this Bricks fellow, I don't want to hear any lip from you either!"

"Here's the deal - we're loaded now. After this blackmail stunt went through we've got a whole truckload of Kornfly cash, but I'm not sure I feel comfortable handing it over to you. After all, $9,000 is a lot of clams. What if you're a flim-flammer? What if you steal it and leave us hanging like a mitten on a meat hook? Dodd's usually too busy shellacking his hair with shoe tar to notice these things, so it's left for me to set things straight, see?"

"So here's the shaboozi - I'm gonna need some proof that this inheritance wad really exists. I want to see a picture of those dollars stacked in a nice tall pile, ya hear, and I'm not gonna shell out any dough until then! So get back to me real quick-like if you know what's good for you. You heard me Williams, hop to it!"

"Sheeeesh, they don't call me a brain genius for nothin'."

-Chippy The Hand

Subject: "They Don't Call Me a Brain Genius For Nothing"? – Good Bye!!!!
From: unionattorney_chamber01@yahoo.com

"Chippy", if that's what you call yourself, are you trying to mock at me? Are you saying I don`t know what I am doing? Do you think this is a childs play?

If you think this is not a legit transaction, please forget it, I have other legal matters that I am treating. In fact, I am ashamed that I made contact with you in the first case!!!

You should know I have never been involved in any illegal matter because I have a reputation to secure. And because you yelled at me, **I WILL ADVICE YOU TO DECLINE THIS VERY TRANSACTION AND LET THE MONEY BE CONSFICATED!!**

- Raymond Williams "Esq"

Subject: I Am *Sooooooooooooooo* Sorry
From: TheHandsMan@gmail.com

Dear Mr. Williams.

Please sir, I am so sorry for the way Chippy spoke to you. I swear he didn't mean it. He just gets a little pent up when he has too many Ring-Dings. I can assure you I had stern words with him and so did Mother. You won't be hearing from his big mouth any time soon. "Isn't that right Chippy?"

"Can it Dodd you're worthless and ya' smell like Mr. Roger's goddamn loafer closet. What is that…camphor?"

"Chippy! I thought you promised to speak nicely from now on? Didn't I tell you Mr. Williams means business here?"

"Look, you're wearing me out like cat fur on a Danish whore. Who gives a shit about this Williams guy anyway? Frankly, I think he's a con job, a real Slick Willie."

"Chippy! We've talked about this. Every time something good happens to us you always ruin it with your foul behavior. Mr. Williams is a very respectable man and he doesn't need to hear your mouth."

"Look, Dodd, I'm a freaking hand puppet, I do what I want, see? If I wanna toss back a bottle of Jack, smoke some stogies and play Candyland with a freakin' blow torch I'll do it, ok? No two-bit lawyer's gonna shut me down. Now, if you'll kindly get your fist out of my crack, I think it's about time for my foot rub. You heard me wigboy, start rubbing or I'm gonna tell Mother you keep candied figs in your underwear!"

- "Ok…"

- "Ok what?"

- "Ok sir…"

- "That's better."

P.S. Mr. Williams, I'm sorry about Chippy's outburst. I swear on a stack of bibles I will send the money, I have it right here under my bed. We just need to see a picture of the inheritance money first. I'm afraid Chippy is insisting on it. He says if you don't send a picture he's going to take that $8,819 and spend it on a trip to Hot Springs. Mr. Williams, I think he's serious. He's already packing a bag.

- Dodd

Subject: Let Him Spend The Money The Way He Wants!!!!!!
From: unionattorney_chamber01@yahoo.com

Norman,

Don't you have any idealogy that this picture of the funds can not be seen because the money of Michael Dodd is in the bank, not my house!   Can't you understand this, or are you trying to aggravate my anger?

Please, if this so called "Chippy" wants to see a picture of the funds, he should just go ahead and see a picture of a river!!!

And your statement "Mr. Williams, I think he's serious." What's serious Norman is that your partner is crazy and you are both fools!

And one more thing Norman, I have told you early on that you should keep this very transaction to yourself. I do not know why your so call "Chippy" continues mailing me through your mailbox. How come this Chippy is entitled to your password????

I have told you before, if you are not interesting in paying the probate office to proceed with your inheritance, please decline yourself in this very transaction!!

Go ahead, let him take $8,819 and spend it on a trip to Hot Springs! It's none of my business. That is your headache!!!!

- Raymond Williams "Esq"

Subject: Ok, Here's The Thing…
From: TheHandsMan@gmail.com

Mr. Williams, we really do want to pay the fee and get our inheritance, but I might as well tell you straight out…Chippy has already spent half the probate money on a reservation at Valley of the Vapors Spa in Arkansas. He says he needs a little R&R and the only way he can get that is with a "full oil rubdown and a crap-load of mountain vapors."

Do you think there's any way we could go down on the price a little? I'm sure the probate office wouldn't mind. Maybe they've got a special rate?

P.S. To answer your question, I'm not sure how Chippy knows my password. I also don't know how he types considering he doesn't have any arms.

- Norman

Subject: You Are A Fool !!!!
From: unionattorney_chamber01@yahoo.com

Norman, why are you playing with yourself? You are a fool if you do not know how your partner got your password for your private box. How old are you????

Do you think probate doesn't know what they are doing? Don't you know I am not in a position to answer your stupid questions? If you can explain to them your present situation, fine. But as for me, I have nothing to tell the probate on your behalf. NOTHING!

If you like, go to the Vapors Spa. I do not care. What concerns me is that I am not you!!!!!

I will advice you Norman, you should not contact me again. **PLEASE, I AM BEGGING YOU IN THE NAME OF GOD, AND I MEAN MY WORD. NEVER!**

- Raymond Williams "Esq"

Subject: WHAT?????
From: TheHandsMan@gmail.com

Mr. Williams,

I'm sorry you're so sensitive about Chippy, but just because he's a hand puppet doesn't mean he's without feelings you know. Your words really hurt us. Next time try picking on someone your own size. Not a 4 ounce hand puppet made out of a handkerchief!

- Dodd

Subject: Look Norman, You Must Seclude Your Chippy Out Of This
From: unionattorney_chamber01@yahoo.com

Dear Norman,

It is not that I am trying to yell at you or make things difficult. It is just that you surprise me because you don't know this so-called "Chippy" is causing a fiasco to you.

I told you before you should not even let your closest friend know about this project because they will be jealous and when this money is transfered to you they will try and have the lions share. Don't you think at all? Don't you know the enemy is living with you?

Norman, you have to seclude your partner in this very transaction. I am beginning to have fear in my mind that when the money is transferred he will harm you. And please Norman, always pray now before going to bed because this is a lot of money we are talking about.

I am now waiting to hear that you have sent the money to the probate, ok?

Raymond Williams "Esq"

Subject: Oh My God, You Were Right!!!!!
From: TheHandsMan@gmail.com

Mr. Williams,

I'm having a very hard time coming to terms with this but you were right about Chippy. I think he's been conspiring against me. He looks at me funny when I'm trying to sleep and lately he's been coy around steak knives. He's even threatening to tell Mother about my secret hiding place if I don't stop "being so squeeze-ass about everything." I really think he may be planning something evil to get that inheritance money.

I can't stand it any longer. I must do something before it's too late. I'll take care of that no-good little snot rag if it's the last thing I do!

BELIEVE ME SIR…NORMAN DODD IS NO FOOL!

Subject: URGENT!
From: unionattorney_chamber01@yahoo.com

Norman, how are you today?

I am so impressed that you knew all along your brother was not happy with you. Now I want you to complete this transaction quickly because I have other cases to handle.

I want you to send the money to the probate office because I hate an improper delay and I don't want a serious matter which I can not handle.

Norman, you know what I'm talking about? **SEND THE MONEY NOW.**

- Raymond Williams "Esq"

Subject: I GOT HIM MR.WILLIAMS!!!!!
From: TheHandsMan@gmail.com

OH I GOT HIM ALRIGHT! I GOT HIM GOOD!!! YOU'RE NOT GONNA HEAR ANY MORE LIP FROM THAT TWO-BIT BACKSTABBING HANDPUPPET!! NO SIR!!

NOW THAT INHERITANCE MONEY IS MINE!! *ALLLLLLLLLLLLL MINE!*

I'm feeling kinda dizzy Mr. Williams…I think I need a chair…and a glass of juice….and maybe a band-aid…

MR. WILLIAMS… I DID A BAD THING…PLEASE… ***DON'T TELL MOTHER!!!!***

Notes

Chapter 1. Svetlana Petrokov

1. **cocktail, polonium-210,** pg. 21 Deadly poison commonly used in espionage (a.k.a. "The Cancer Master"). Contains 1 part vermouth, 2 parts Crème de Cassis, 4 parts crushed ice (chipped if you're Chechen), and 1 splash polonium. (Be cautious not to spill on skin or clothing as disintegration may occur.)

2. **chimpanzees, Russian space,** pg. 23 Trained for intergalactic travel and light mopping, these primates may be rented hourly at the Русская станция космоса (Chimpatorium) in Minsk. (Rates include a jug of Tang and 1 pair of regulation-style chimp mittens.)

3. **Sovietski, Hotel,** pg. 25 Located at 32 Leningradskii Prospekt in downtown Moscow. Room charge includes electric clock and 1 roll of government issued toilet paper. (Note: For proper service, it is advisable to leave Ivan the desk attendant a generous supply of potato vodka and a set of lacquered nesting dolls. Also, never ring for fresh towels after midnight without proper paperwork.)

4. **nitrobenzene, the hair-melting qualities of,** pg. 27 Also known as "Oil of Mirbane" and "Diet Cherry Coke." When suffering from a severe chemical burn it is helpful to 1. clean wound of all detritus 2. reflect on inner strengths 3. keep screaming to a minimum. 4. see number 3.

Chapter 2. Fudgey Carmichael

1. **Crablake, Candace** pg. 38 C-level actress known for her roles in *Wonder Girl and Wanda*, *Death Takes a Taxi*, and *Jell-O Wrestling Sluts of Lower Melrose*. Died in June, 2007 in a bizarre pudding accident. Details remain unclear, although foul play is suspected.

2. **Arthur, Bea,** pg. 39 Star of the hit television shows *Maude* and *The Golden Girls*. Bea Arthur was thrown off the set of the reality TV show, *Hey, Show Me Somethin'!* for punching a stage hand in the mouth. The argument was allegedly over "what's better - boxers or briefs?"

3. **Aames, Willie** pg. 47   Former television star famous for his role as the curly-haired teenager in that show about a whole shit load of kids living in a big white house. Aames is now a born again Christian - no kidding. See *Bibleman* episodes 1-4.

4. **twins, the Mackel** pg. 47   Fletcher and Travers Mackel are identical twin news broadcasters for WDSU in New Orleans. It's unreported how they feel about fried pies, but it would be poor journalism not to mention Fletcher's obsession with mincemeat.

5. **date, alley**, pg. 52   A popular means of acquiring sex for cash. (a.k.a. "Darkened Hand Whammy," "The 3 A.M. Palm Brigade," "Blow Job Behind Chung Ho Pang," and "Hey, What The Hell Are You Doing?") Source: *Encyclopedia of Acquiring Sex for Cash* 1997.

Chapter 3. Phebus McPhadden

1. **otters, corn,** pg. 62   There is no such thing as corn otters. There is also no such thing as Triple-Breasted Swamp Beavers but try not to let that spoil your hunting fun.

2. **wombats, the ears of**, pg. 69 It is a federal offense to de-ear a wombat, but if you must, you must. Begin by sharpening a large knife (not a paring knife, more like a bear-hunting knife) then cut at the base, peel off, and discard into a handy receptacle. There. Now are you happy?

3. **Irish money, filthy**, pg. 70 Ireland has replaced their filthy old bank notes with bright, shiny euros which are not only clean and sparkly but scented with the lush, green man fur of Liam Neeson.

Chapter 4.   Demetrius Chilblain

1. **phrenology, (skullmapping)** pg. 84 Theory that determines personality traits based on the lumps on one's head (i.e. the benevolent lump, the avarice lump, the murderous lump, and the "mystery lump" which modern doctors sometimes refer to as "the nose.")

2. **Burr, Raymond**, pg. 88 Overweight actor famous for popular television series *Ironside*. Not to be confused with former vice-president and knife-wielding psychopath, Aaron Burr, killer of Alexander Hamilton, J.F.K. and Bambi's mother.

3. **squid, fear of giant,** pg. 91 (a.k.a. cephalophobia) An uncommon psychological disorder suffered by such notable personalities as Albert Einstein, Golda Mier, Robert Stack, Juggy Gales and Diana Grove. Fear of developing this disorder is known as cephalophobia-phobia.

4. **Queen, Her Majesty the**, pg. 94 Antiquated British figurehead known for her icy countenance and ungainly hats. Often spotted waving at crowds, randomly and for no apparent reason (could be due to drunkenness). Source: *Teeth, Tea and Tippling: A True History of the British Isles* (pamphlet found in a bathroom stall at Heathrow Airport).

Chapter 5. Bradlowe Crumley

1. **organs, sale of human,** pg. 108 The human organ trade is a lucrative business in developing nations superseded only by the sale of Somalian eye patches and Chinese chestal wigs.

2. **Guyana, (not Ghana)** pg. 112 Common clerical error in the travel industry. If you find you are in Guyana instead of Ghana you might as well stay. Where else are you going to find a mutton taco for 12 cents?

3. **monopurse, suffering from**, pg. 113 This word does not exist in the English language - until now. Perhaps the fraudster was referring to "monopode," a creature having only one foot, or "mini purse," a very, very small purse.

Chapter 6. Dr. Bifida Hendrix M.D.

1. **Everett, Chad (fan club)** pg. 122 There is no known Chad Everett Fan club. If you'd like to start one, why not host your first meeting on his front lawn, 5472 Island Forest Place, Westlake Village, CA. (Caution: watch out for Nurse Bascomb and the moat of feral wolves.)

2. **spinal column, bifurcated (i.e. duospinosis)** pg. 122 Spinal bifurcation is a painful disorder resulting in the growth of two spines (commonly found in the backs of waifs, miscreants, and roustabouts.) The only treatment to date is the application of Dr.Bifida Hendrix's Vertibrizer. Source: Bifida Hendrix M.D.

3. **theme funeral, Disney**, pg. 148 Putting the "fun" back in funeral since 1971. For details on having your own Disney-themed funeral contact the Walt Disney World Funerary Division in Orlando, Florida, 407-939-6244. (Make sure to request 6 Goofy pallbearers "at no extra cost." Code word: "embalmerific!")

Chapter 7. Danny Wingnuts

1. **sandwich, crap,** pg. 162 A situation deemed an utter failure often involving anything Wingnut related. Includes shame, loathing, and a sickening sense of doom. (Does not include frizzle stick or bag of chips.)

2. **spooge, lung,** pg. 162 Substance emitted from the lungs when "paint huffing" occurs. In texture it can resemble anything from whipped beets to liquefied polyester. If you should encounter an individual suffering from such a condition, roll them over and poke them with a stick. If death ensues, cease poking.

3. **Wingnut Way, The,** pg. 163 Similar to "The Wingnut Vision," "The Wingnut Advantage" and "Wingnuts Gone Wild." All of which end up a gigantic crap sandwich.

4. **shit, kicking the living (out of),** pg. 170 Act of beating someone within an inch of their life. Is considered justifiable if "stratification" or "The Wingnut Vision" are not properly implemented. Also acceptable if one is caught besmirching the name of the Pittsburgh Steelers.

Chapter 8. Junior Samples Jr.

1. **whack, skull,** pg. 174 A homemade variety of corn whiskey (a.k.a.: white lightnin', pop skull, bush whiskey, throat paint, stump hole, ruckus juice, mule kick, happy Sally, old horsey, and sweet spirits of cats-a-fightin'). Source: *The Junior Samples Museum Guide* pg. 1-12.

2. **Foible, Ford,** pg. 194 Built in 1982 to replace the Ford Fracas, the Foible originally had dual suspension and a detachable rumble seat. Unfortunately, the rumble seat contained the crank shaft, ignition and most of the wheels, so its detachment proved fatal in 3,450 cases in New Jersey alone. It was soon scrapped and replaced with the Ford Fiasco, which, needless to say, had its own problems.

Chapter 9. Opus Knight

1. **Boot, The Holy,** pg. 185 Justin Calf Roping Boot size 8 ½. Does not hold any mystical powers of prognostication. Does smell bad and look ridiculous with a sundress.

2. **rigamarolery**, pg. 188 The act of rigamarolling. Something one does when dawdling, dilly-dallying, and dorking around just aren't good enough. (From the Latin *riga:* to jack around, and *marolling:* pretty much all of the time.)

3. **magnaboots,** pg. 192 These multi-colored, magnet-soled boots not only improve one's electrical conductivity but also collect small bits of metal and pocket change from the sides of most highways. (Should be worn with caution near semi trucks, cranes and other high-powered machinery.)

Chapter 10. Steve Teufelman

1. **stuff, sticky,** pg. 210 Any fluid akin to blood, semen, saliva, mucus or other human substances that prompt police officers to wear rubber gloves and look uncomfortable.

2. **woodlock,** pg. 211 Word unknown in the English language. May be a Nigerian colloquialism for "jackass" or "total fucking moron."

Chapter 11. Norman Dodd

1. **Spaniard, The Drunken**, pg. 220 Popular party trick involving 1 Spaniard and a cup of gin. May involve ping pong balls and support hose if performed by a schizophrenic with "mother issues."

2. **loafer closet, Mr. Roger's goddamned**, (smelling like) pg. 229 Actually, child educator Fred Roger's loafer closet was always "neat and fresh-smelling" according to his *co- stars and was only occasionally "befouled by the stench of soiled sneakers." Source: paper mache hand puppet, King Friday, PBS, 1979.

Addendum: (via cell phone interview) "Meow, meow, meow, goddamned loafer closet, meow, meow." - Henrietta Pussycat.

3. **mountain vapors, crap-load of,** pg. 231 Excellent source of relaxation for combating schizophrenia and various impulse control disorders. Also a suitable environment for "getting your stiff on and unloading on a freakin' mountain bush." – Chippy The Hand.

Cast Bios

I'd like to thank the people who posed as characters for this book. All photographs were taken in New Orleans, LA.

Jeremy Johnson (Dr. Bifida Hendrix M.D.)

Jeremy is the lead singer for the rock band, *Good Guys*, and a videographer for *Comic Relief*. He doesn't often dress as a woman, but if he did, he'd have to shave three times – once up, twice down. Jeremy looks alarmingly good in an orange pantsuit.

Demian Estevez (Steve, Paco, Cosmologist #2)

Demian owns Mojo Coffee House at 1500 Magazine Street – a place filled with colorful characters who don't seem to mind being humiliated in book form. When in town, make sure to stop by for a beverage from "the crazy Guatemalan." (Demian also looks good in a pantsuit, especially if it has dramatic side vents.)

Angela Estevez (Velma, Brenda, Cosmologist #4)

Angee has a perfectly straight spine and to the best of her knowledge she has never dated a serial killer. Although she did recently have a Day of the Dead-themed wedding with Demian Estevez, which is odd, considering her obsession with all things Norwegian. (Note: wedding gifts can be Scandinavian in nature but should not include dried fish or underage porn.)

C.J. Hauser (Little Billy)

C.J. is 11-years old and still alive, so if you were planning on sending his mother Angee a sympathy card, don't bother. When he's not pretending to have two tail bones, he enjoys video games and reading Edgar Allen Poe.

Brett Ruth (Demetrius Chilblain)

Brett is a former mathematician and current owner of the five-star bed and breakfast, The McKendrick-Breaux House, which is also the childhood home of T-Bone Burnett. Brett has no fear of driving a car or cephalopods and has even been known to eat them from time to time (the squid, not the cars).

Jeremy Young (Phebus and Bill)

Jeremy has been a cook at the Ritz Carlton and on several oil rigs and he can filet a flounder with a tin can. To date, he has never stuffed a wombat, although if asked for a recipe, he'd probably recommend cornbread and crude oil.

Randy Muller (Carlos)

Randy is an artist and avid skateboarder. He creates drawings in graphite and tattoo ink on pretty much anything that will sit still. For his 28th birthday he sat still enough for his parents to tattoo their signatures on his left thigh. He advises against huffing Krylon and other synthetic propellants…most of the time.

Chrispin Barnes (Bradlowe, Cosmologist #3)

Chrispin is a freelance videographer and also provided much of the Photoshop work for this book. Although he has never been to Africa, he has hitchhiked the majority of the continental U.S. and all with just two kidneys. Chrispin had Randy tattoo nuclear waste on his right tricep.

Randy Morrison (Norman Dodd)

Randy Morrison is a designer and sculptor of Mardi Gras floats. His work is in private collections, theme parks, casinos, hotels, and Hollywood films. He is not schizophrenic, nor does he keep hand puppets. He's also never performed "The Triple Kitten Toss" at Club Titters, but has expressed interest.

Bill Chott (Jr. Samples Jr.)

Bill is a professional actor who has appeared in numerous movies, television shows, and stage performances including "The Ringer," "Saturday Night Live," and "The Dana Carvey Show." Unlike the rest of us, he actually gets paid to dress up and act silly. If you don't believe me visit him at TheImprovTrick.com

Vera Lukas (Rhonda)

Originally from Germany, Vera is a belly dancer, professional dog trainer, and aromatherapist. She is so talented in these fields, in the future she will likely produce a dancing schnauzer that smells faintly of bayberries. (By the way, she has no idea where to find an incinerator in Syracuse, but if you want your dog trained visit Bark4Vera.com.)

Fudgey Carmichael (Himself)

Fudgey is still going to auditions but has yet to land any roles. Although he did recently try out for the part of "bystander #2" in the reality TV show, *Does This Thing Make You Itch?* In the meantime, Fudgey works the dough hopper at Hubig's Pies. If you'd like to be his friend or finance his next monster movie visit him at myspace.com/FudgeyCarmichael.

Diana Grove (Svetlana Petrokov, Mrs. Chilblain, Mrs. Wainwright, and Sharon Mincemeyer's right hand)

Diana writes letters to con men and hope they write back. If you email her a "lucrative business proposal with big cash rewards," she'll probably respond as a reference librarian with a trick knee and a syphilitic monkey.

Todd Grove (Opus Knight, Agent Y, The Svetlana Suit 3000, Demetrius' right arm, "Mr. Gabriel's" legs, and Danny Wingnuts)

Todd Grove produces live comedy events and lives with Diana Grove. He is frightened by his pictures in this book.

Made in the USA